✳ THIS BOOK ✳

_____

_____

_____

_____

THE LION ILLUSTRATED BIBLE
FOR CHILDREN

Give thanks to the Lord, because he is good;
 his love is everlasting. . . .
He alone performs great miracles;
 his love is everlasting.
By his wisdom he made the heavens;
 his love is everlasting;
he built the earth on the deep waters;
 his love is everlasting. . . .
He did not forget us when we were defeated;
 his love is everlasting;
he freed us from our enemies;
 his love is everlasting.
He gives food to every living creature;
 his love is everlasting.
Give thanks to the God of heaven;
 his love is everlasting.

Psalm 136:1, 4–6, 23–26

THE LION

ILLUSTRATED

BIBLE

FOR CHILDREN

Retold by

LOIS ROCK

Illustrated by

CHRISTINA BALIT

LION
CHILDREN'S

To my wonderful parents,
Mama and Derek,
Poppie and Kiki C.B.

To John and Linda,
and all those you love L.R.

Text by Lois Rock
Illustrations copyright © 2001 Christina Balit
This edition copyright © 2005 Lion Hudson
Book design by Nicky Jex

The moral rights of the author and illustrator
have been asserted

A Lion Children's Book
an imprint of
Lion Hudson plc
Mayfield House, 256 Banbury Road,
Oxford OX2 7DH, England
www.lionhudson.com
ISBN 0 7459 4936 3

First published in 2001 under the title
The Lion Bible: Everlasting Stories
This revised edition 2005
10 9 8 7 6 5 4 3 2 1 0

Acknowledgments
Scriptures on pp. 23, 27, 35, 71, 72, 84, 111, 129,
135, 139, 153, 160, 163, 171 and 194 quoted from
the Good News Bible published by The Bible Societies/
Harper Collins Publishers Ltd, UK © American Bible
Society 1966, 1971, 1976, 1992, used with permission.
The Scripture quotations contained on pp. 16, 30,
107 and 158 are from The New Revised Standard
Version of the Bible, Anglicized Edition, copyright ©
1989, 1995 by the Division of Christian Education of
the National Council of the Churches of Christ in the
United States of America, and are used by permission.
All rights reserved. Bible extracts on pp. 141 and 179
(slightly adapted) from The Jerusalem Bible © 1966
by Darton, Longman & Todd Ltd and Doubleday &
Company, Inc. Used by permission of Darton,
Longman & Todd Ltd, and Doubleday, a division of
Random House, Inc.

A catalogue record for this book is available
from the British Library

Typeset in Lapidary 333 BT
Printed and bound in Singapore

Contents

Introduction   10

The Old Testament   13

The Making of the World   14
The World Is Filled with Creatures   16

The Story of the Garden of Eden   18
The Tree of Knowledge   20
Beyond the Garden   22

The Story of the Flood   24
The Flood Rises   26
The Flood Falls   29
The Promise of the Rainbow   30

Abraham and the Covenant   32
Abraham and Isaac   34
Isaac and His Twin Sons   36
Jacob's Dream   38
Jacob and the Trickster   40
Jacob and Esau   42

The Story of Joseph   44
Joseph Is Sold   46
Joseph the Slave   48
Joseph and the Pharaoh   51
Joseph Meets His Brothers   52
Joseph and Benjamin   54

The Great Exodus   56
The Baby Moses   58
Moses and His People   60
Moses and the Burning Bush   62
Moses Goes to the Pharaoh   64
The Stubborn Pharaoh   66
The Passover   68
Crossing the Red Sea   71

Wanderings in the Wilderness   72
The Great Commandments   74
Obedience and Disobedience   76
The Death of Moses   78

The Story of Joshua   80
Spies   83
Into Canaan   84
The Battle of Jericho   86

The Stories of the Heroes   88
Gideon and the Midianites   90
Samson the Strong   92
Samson's Final Victory   95

The Story of Ruth   96

The Story of Samuel   98

The Story of the Great Kings   100
Saul the Warrior   102
David and Goliath   104
David the Outlaw   106
David the King   108
David and Bathsheba   110
Solomon the Wise   112
Solomon's Temple   114

The Story of the Northern Kingdom   116
Elijah and the Fire from Heaven   118
Ahab and the Vineyard   120
The Chariot of Fire   123
The Miracles of Elisha   124
Jehu's Wild Ride   126
The Faithful Prophet   128

The Story of Jonah   130
Jonah and the Castor Oil Plant   132

The Story of the Southern Kingdom   134
The Siege of Jerusalem   136
The Fall of Jerusalem   138

The Story of the Jews in Exile   140
Daniel in the Pit of Lions   142

The Story of the Returning Exiles   144

The Story of Esther   146
Mordecai and Haman   148

The New Testament 151

The Story of the Birth of Jesus 152
Mary, Joseph, and the Dream 154
The Stable in Bethlehem 156
The Shepherds and the Angels 158
Old Simeon 160
Jealous King Herod 162
The Wise Men Find Jesus 164
The Escape to Egypt 166

The Story of the Boy Jesus 168

The Story of John 170

The Story of Jesus the Teacher 172
Water and Wine 174
The Two House Builders 176
The Prayer 178
Wind and Waves 180
The Beloved Daughter 182
  The Miraculous Food 184
  The Lost Sheep 186
  The Parable of the Good Samaritan 188
  The Prodigal Son 190
  Jesus and the Children 193

The Story of Jesus in Jerusalem 194
Jesus and the Temple Merchants 196
Jesus and the Great Commandment 198
The Betrayal 201

The Story of the Crucifixion 202
The Tomb 204

The Story of the Resurrection 206
Doubting Thomas 208
Jesus and Peter 210
Jesus Is Taken Up to Heaven 212
The Day of Pentecost 214

Index of Bible References 217

Index of People from the Bible 220

Introduction

❦

The Bible is the book of the Christian faith, of the followers of Jesus. In its pages, they say, can be found understanding and wisdom: companions for the journey of life.

Much of the Bible is made up of stories. Some are happy, others are sad; some are straightforward, others are perplexing; some are homely, others are full of mystery and miracle. All have captivated listeners for hundreds of generations.

From the Bible comes a story of the making of the world—a world that God created, good and perfect; and a story of a paradise garden in which people could live as friends of God. It is followed all too soon by the story of how evil came into that world, and of how people turned away from God, choosing instead the ways of wickedness and violence.

Then, emerging from the mists of time, come stories that are set in the ancient civilizations of the Bronze age four thousand years ago. They begin with the story of a man named Abraham, whom God chose to be the father of a great nation. God tells him that his descendants are to be a blessing to all the world, but their story is a puzzling one. Over the following hundreds of years come tales of great leaders—prophets and teachers—who bring the words that tell the people plainly how to live as God's people and walk the way of peace and justice. Yet throughout there are stories that are all too recognizably human—stories of treachery as well as loyalty, deceit as well as honesty, fighting as well as peace.

In the Bible, it becomes clear that Abraham's descendants, who become known as the Jewish people, long to be free of all the wickedness that defeats them and drags them down. Their prophets begin to speak of a new promise:

God will send a leader greater than any other who will enable them truly to live as God's people.

Then comes the story of an angel announcing to a young woman that she will bear a special child—a son whom she must call Jesus, who will be known as the Son of the Most High God.

The life of Jesus changed the course of world history. He told people that God's way was the way of love and forgiveness, and stories of his miracles tell of the healing he brought to those who were sick or downhearted. Some were angry about Jesus' teachings and had him put to death . . . but soon his friends were talking of his being alive again, and proclaiming that God's love was stronger than all the wickedness and violence that had been in the world since the time people first turned away from their Maker.

And so the many stories within the Bible become part of one great story— a story that encompasses all that is good and all that is bad within humankind, and points to a God of unfailing forgiveness and everlasting love.

The Old Testament

The first section of the Bible is known as the Old Testament. It is a collection of some forty ancient books, the oldest of which may have been written down over two thousand five hundred years ago, and the most recent, only a little more than two thousand years ago. The books are the special writings of the Jewish people and were written in their language, called Hebrew (except for small parts of later books which were written in a language called Aramaic). Although the very first manuscripts no longer exist, the Jewish people have always made careful copies, and some of the oldest fragments of those are nearly two thousand years old.

Some of the stories appear to have been part of a storytelling tradition, with the ancient tales handed down from one generation to another long before they were written down. Others are more clearly rooted in history. In the various books, the reader will find all sorts of writing: stories, history, lists of laws, wise sayings, words spoken by the prophets, poems and hymns. The following selection of stories includes glimpses of all these kinds of writing.

The Making of the World

From ancient times, people have looked at the immensity of the world around them and wondered how it all began. The first book of the Bible, the book of Genesis, begins with ancient stories of creation that seek to give an answer.

In the beginning, God created the universe.

At that time, the earth had no shape. It was a great emptiness, engulfed in the deepest darkness of a raging ocean.

The power of God was moving over the water.

Then God spoke: "Let there be light." And there was light, and it was good in every way. God divided the darkness and the light, and God called the darkness "night," and the light "day." Evening passed and morning came. The first day was over.

Then God spoke: "Let there be a sky reaching as a dome across the universe." And there was sky, and it was good in every way. Evening passed and morning came. The second day was over.

Then God spoke: "Let the waters be gathered into seas and let dry land appear." And so it was, and the sea and the earth were good in every way.

Then God spoke: "Let there be plants of every kind—those that bear grain and those that bear fruit." So the earth produced plants, and they were good in every way. Evening passed and morning came. The third day was over.

Then God spoke: "Let there be lights in the sky to mark the day and the night and seasons of the year." And so it was. God made the sun to shine in the day and the moon at night. God also made the stars. Everything was good in every way. Evening passed and morning came. The fourth day was over.

The World Is Filled with Creatures

Then God spoke: "Let the waters be filled with living things and let the air be thronged with birds." And so it was. God made the creatures of the sea and birds of every kind. They were good in every way. Evening passed and morning came. The fifth day was over.

Then God spoke: "Let there be all kinds of animals." And so there were. Then God said, "Now we will make human beings to take care of this world that is so good in every way." The people had the likeness of God, and they were given God's lovely world in which to live. God was very pleased. Evening passed and morning came. The sixth day was over.

So the whole universe was complete. By the seventh day, God had finished. God rested; God blessed the seventh day and set it apart as a special day. And that is how the universe was created.

The earth is the Lord's and all that is in it,
the world, and those who live in it;
for he has founded it on the seas,
and established it on the rivers.

Psalm 24:1–2

The Story of the Garden of Eden

*The second story in the Bible tells of the creation of the world
in a different way. It also tells of how the first man and the first
woman disobeyed God and in so doing let loose all the power of evil.*

When God made the universe, there were no plants. No seeds had
sprouted, for no rain had ever fallen, nor was there anyone to till the
ground. From time to time, a mist rose from beneath the surface and watered
the land.

Then God took some soil and formed a man out of it. He breathed into the
man's nostrils, and the man began to live.

Then God planted a garden in Eden, in the East. It was filled with beautiful
trees that gave good fruit. In the middle of the garden stood the tree of life and
the tree that gives knowledge of what is good and what is bad.

God placed the man in the Garden of Eden, so that it would be a home for him. "Take care of this place," said God, "and it will provide you with all you need. Only take care not to eat the fruit from the tree that gives knowledge of what is good and what is bad, for if you do, you will die."

Then God said, "It is not good for the man to be alone. I must provide a companion for him." So God took soil from the ground and formed all the animals and all the birds. He brought them to the man and asked him to name them.

So it was that the man named all the animals and all the birds, but among the creatures there was none that would be a help and companion.

Then God caused the man to fall into a deep sleep, and while he was sleeping, God took a rib from the man's side and formed it into a woman.

When the man saw the woman God had made, he knew he had found a true companion. "Here at last is one of my own kind," he said, "bone of my bone, and flesh of my flesh."

The man and the woman delighted in being together, unembarrassed and unafraid.

The Tree of Knowledge

Now the snake was the most cunning animal that God had made.

One day, the snake slithered close to the woman as she sat in the garden. "There is a question I wish to ask you," it whispered in a thin, shivery voice. "Did God really tell you not to eat fruit from any tree in the garden?"

"We may eat the fruit from any tree," the woman replied confidently, "except the tree in the middle. God told us not to eat from its fruit—not even to touch it—or we will die."

The snake shook with silent laughter. "That's not true. God only said that to deceive you, because if you eat from it you will become like God, knowing both what is good and what is bad."

The woman looked at the tree with new eyes. How beautiful it is, she said to herself, how lovely the fruit looks. As she gazed on it, a new longing grew within her. How wonderful it would be to become wise, she thought.

So she took some of the fruit and ate it. Then she gave some to the man and he ate, too.

As soon as they had eaten, they realized they were naked, and at once they were embarrassed. So they took fig leaves and covered themselves.

In the cool of the evening, God came walking in the garden. The man and the woman hid among the trees. But God had come looking for them. "Where are you?" God called.

The man answered, "I heard you coming, and I was afraid. I hid from you because I was naked."

"Who told you that?" God asked, and God's voice was sad. "Did you eat the fruit from the forbidden tree?"

"The woman gave me some of its fruit," said the man, "the woman you gave me as my companion."

God turned to the woman. "Why did you do this?"

With her head hanging down, she replied, "The snake tricked me."

Beyond the Garden

Then God spoke to the snake: "You have done great harm, and for this you must be punished. From now on, you will crawl on your belly, and you will eat dust as long as you live. You will be hated by people. They will trample on your head, and you will bite their heels with poison in your teeth."

Next, God spoke to the woman: "Now you will suffer pain. Childbirth will be hard and difficult, and the gentle friendship with your husband will be spoiled."

Finally, God spoke to the man: "You, too, have disobeyed me, and the earth itself will be cursed for your disobedience. You will have to toil hard to make it produce crops; weeds and thorns will grow up rampant and strong, and choke the plants you need. Then, after a lifetime of weary work, you will die, and your body will return to the soil from which you were formed."

The man, Adam, named his wife Eve, for she was the mother of all. God made Adam and Eve clothes out of animal skins and sent them out of the Garden of Eden.

Then to the east side of the garden, God sent mighty winged creatures and a flaming sword that turned in all directions. Now no one was allowed near the tree of life—for those who ate its fruit would live forever.

From the depths of my despair
   I call to you, Lord.
Hear my cry, O Lord;
   listen to my call for help!
If you kept a record of our sins,
   who could escape being condemned?
But you forgive us,
   so that we should stand in awe of you.

I wait eagerly for the Lord's help,
   and in his word I trust.
I wait for the Lord
    more eagerly than watchmen wait
     for the dawn—
   than watchmen wait for the dawn.

Psalm 130:1–6

The Story of the Flood

The story of Adam and Eve tells how evil came into the world. The ancient
text says that from that moment on wickedness increased. God saw the evil
and sent a great flood to wash it away.

❧

Adam and Eve had children. After many generations, their descendants filled all the world.

God looked out upon the people. Their deeds were wicked. Their thoughts were wicked. God was filled with deep regret. "I will wipe out these people I have created," said God, "and I will wipe out the animals and the birds. I am sorry I ever made them."

Only one man pleased God, and that was Noah. "I am going to wipe out the world," God told him. "Build for yourself a special boat—a giant box, a mighty ark. Make it out of good timber and put rooms in it. Cover it with tar inside and out. Build it with three decks and put a door in the side. Everything on the earth will be destroyed, but I am going to make a special agreement with you." So Noah did as God said.

God spoke again: "Noah, take into the ark those whom I want to save. Take your wife and your three sons and your sons' wives.

"Take also with you a male and female of every kind of animal and bird. Of some, take seven pairs; of others, just one pair. Do this so that every species will survive and will bear young on earth again."

And so Noah did.

The Flood Rises

Noah went into the ark with his family and with the animals and birds. Seven days later, the flood came.

Water fell from the sky in torrents, and it did not cease for forty days. The flood rose up from the ground. The ark began to float.

The water became deeper and still deeper. Soon it covered the mountains, and still it went on rising. Every living creature that remained on the earth died. Only those who sheltered with Noah in the wooden ark were safe.

There they stayed, for a hundred and fifty days.

Lord, your constant love reaches the heavens;
  your faithfulness extends to the skies.
Your righteousness is towering like the mountains;
  your justice is like the depths of the sea.
People and animals are in your care.

Psalm 36:5—6

The Flood Falls

God had not forgotten Noah and the animals in the ark. After many days had passed, God sent a wind. The storm clouds blew away, and the water no longer welled up from the deep. Slowly, slowly, the flood waters ebbed away.

At length, the ark came to rest on a mountaintop in the range known as Ararat. Still the waters went down, till at last the tops of the mountains appeared.

Forty days later, Noah opened a window and sent out a raven. It did not come back, but flew over the earth till the waters had gone.

Then Noah sent out a dove. It could not find anywhere to land, so it flew back to the ark. Seven days later, Noah sent it out again. It came back in the evening, and in its beak was a fresh olive leaf. Noah was glad, for this was a sure sign that the water had subsided. Seven days later, Noah sent the dove out again, and this time it did not return.

The days went by, and the waters continued to recede, till Noah could see land all around. Then God spoke to him again: "Go out of the ark, you and your wives and your sons and their wives, and set free all the animals and all the birds, so they may have young and spread over all the earth."

And so Noah did.

The Promise of the Rainbow

Then Noah built an altar and gave thanks to God for keeping him safe from the flood. God was pleased with Noah and made this promise: "Never again will I destroy the world in this way. I know that humankind is frail and cannot resist the lure of wickedness. But I promise that for as long as the world exists, there will always be a time for sowing seeds and a time for harvesting crops. There will be cold and heat, summer and winter, day and night.

"All living beings can trust these words. So raise your families, bear your young, and fill the earth with living creatures.

"As a sign of my promise, I will put a rainbow in the sky. Whenever the sky is dark with clouds, and a rainbow arches across them, I will remember what I have said. I will remember my agreement with all living beings, and I will never break it."

Not to us, O Lord, not to us,
but to your name give glory,
for the sake of your steadfast
love and your faithfulness.

Psalm 115:1

Abraham and the Covenant

*The stories at the very beginning of the Bible—including those of Creation
and Noah—belong to the mists of time. Next come stories set firmly in the ancient
Near East—Babylonia, Canaan, and Egypt—in the Bronze Age. They tell the
history of a nation, beginning with the story of Abraham.*

Long ago, in the land of Mesopotamia, lived a man named Abram. He was
married to a woman named Sarai. She was very beautiful, but she was not
able to have children. Both husband and wife lamented their lack of descendants.
Then the God whom Abram called "the Lord" spoke: "Leave your country, your
relatives and your father's home, and go to a land that I am going to show you.
I will give you many descendants, and they will become a great nation. I will bless
you and make your name famous, so that you will be a blessing. . . . And through
you I will bless all the nations."

Abram obeyed. He left his elegant city dwelling and he went with all his
household to the land of Canaan. They lived as nomads among the people there,
setting up their camp of dark, billowing tents wherever they could find pasture
for their flocks of sheep and goats, cattle and donkeys and camels.

The years passed. There were times of hardship and times of abundance, but
through them all, Sarai remained childless. Both husband and wife grew bitter
and disillusioned.

Sometimes it seemed to Abram that he was alone in the world, having to use
every deceit and cunning he could to survive. At other times, he still believed he
heard the Lord speaking to him.

"Listen," said God. "I will make this covenant with you. Your name will no
longer be Abram but Abraham. The very word promises that you will be the
ancestor of many nations. And your wife's name will be Sarah, and she will
become the mother of nations, and there will be kings among her descendants."

So, although he was by now very old, Abraham's hope was renewed. But the
aging Sarah grew more scornful.

"Don't you men understand anything?" she said. "Don't you know that
I am past the years when I can have children? It's time to give up dreaming."

But then, when hope should have died, the Lord's promise came true. Sarah
became pregnant and she bore Abraham a son. The boy was named Isaac, which
means "he laughs." Sarah said, "God has brought me joy and laughter. Everyone
who hears about this will laugh with me."

Abraham and Isaac

Some years after Isaac was born, God tested Abraham.

"Take your son," God said, "your only son whom you love so much. Go to a mountain that I will show you, and there on that mountain, sacrifice him to me."

The following morning, Abraham woke his son brusquely. "Isaac, we must be up and on our way."

"Why, what's happening?" Isaac's eyes were round with wonder.

"It is a day for offering sacrifices to our God. Come! I have gathered wood for the fire, and we must load it onto the donkey."

Isaac felt very proud as he set out with his father and two servants. "You will let me help you, won't you?" asked Isaac eagerly. "I'm big enough to take part, aren't I?"

He looked brightly at his father, then turned away, silent. His father's eyes were shadowy and brooding.

They came to the place for the sacrifice. "Isaac, untie the wood and carry it for me," ordered Abraham. Speaking to the servants, he commanded, "Stay here. We will go on further to worship God, and then we will return."

Abraham took with him a knife and a pot of hot coals to start the fire.

"I see we have everything," said Isaac. "But where is the lamb for the sacrifice?"

"God himself will provide one," answered Abraham grimly.

On the mountain, Abraham built a stone altar and arranged the wood on it. Then he snatched his son, gripped him and bound him, and laid him on top. Isaac watched with wild eyes as his father raised the knife.

But an angel's voice rang out: "Abraham, Abraham!"

"Yes, here I am," Abraham replied.

"Do not hurt the boy. Do not touch him. You have shown that you are ready to obey God."

Abraham looked around. He saw a ram with its horns caught in a bush. With trembling hands, he untied his son and left him, sobbing wretchedly on the ground. Then he went and took the ram, killed it and burned the body on the altar as a sacrifice to God.

As the flames died down, he drew Isaac close to his side. "My son," he said, "in my faltering way, I have always tried to listen to God. Today I have learned something new, and so I will give this place a name to help me remember what that is. I will call this place 'The Lord Provides.' "

"Abraham believed God, and
because of his faith God accepted
him as righteous." And so Abraham
was called God's friend.

James 2:23

Isaac and His Twin Sons

When Isaac was a grown man, Abraham sent a servant back to his own people to seek a bride for him. It was soon arranged for Isaac to marry Rebecca. She bore him twin sons: Esau and Jacob.

Esau, the firstborn of the twins, grew to be a hunter. His father admired him for his skill and was proud of his strong, wild-looking son with streaming red hair and flowing beard. Jacob was different: smooth-skinned, clever with words, and happy to stay at home. Jacob was the one his mother preferred.

One day, when Jacob was cooking bean soup, Esau returned from hunting.

"Let me have some of that soup right now," he growled. "I'm dying of hunger."

"Only if you give me the rights you have as the firstborn son," replied the silver-tongued Jacob.

"All right! If you want them, you can have them. I'll die if I don't eat," grumbled Esau, and he made the promise that Jacob so desired.

Years passed. When Isaac was very old and knew that he would soon die, he called Esau to his side.

"Go hunting, my dear son," he said. "Bring me an animal and cook it for me. Then, after the meal, I will give you my final blessing."

Rebecca overheard this, and when Esau was away, she called Jacob. "Go and fetch two fat young goats from the flock," she whispered to him. "I will cook your father a meal, and you can then take some of it to him, so he will bless you instead. Isaac is blind—he will never notice."

"But he will," Jacob said. "Esau is covered with hair, and my skin is smooth."

"Just do as I say," insisted Rebecca. "If anything goes wrong, I'll take the blame."

Together they prepared the food. Then Rebecca took the skins from the goats and tied them to Jacob's arms and neck.

"Now go, take the meal to Isaac and ask for the blessing," she said.

Isaac was puzzled when he heard Jacob speak, and he asked him to come closer. "I hear Jacob's voice, yet I can feel that these are Esau's arms," he said. "Are you really Esau?"

"I am," Jacob lied easily.

So Isaac gave Jacob his blessing, a blessing for wealth and power.

When Esau returned and found he had been cheated a second time, he was furious. "When my father is dead, I will take my revenge," he said. "I will kill that twisted trickster and be rid of him."

Rebecca heard of his plan. "Go," she warned Jacob. "Run away to my father's people. Stay there till I send word that it is safe to return."

Jacob's Dream

Run! Keep on running. Someone may be following you.

Jacob gasped for breath as he clambered up the rocky hillside. Fear was urging him on . . . telling him to keep moving, to go a little faster.

He reached the top and looked back. "Good-bye," he said, "to the land that was my home." Sadly, he began the descent on the other side, slithering over pebbles, ignoring the briars that tore at the hem of his garment and clawed at his feet. He was anxious to keep moving while it was still light.

Yet, as the sun sank to a blood-red arc on the horizon, Jacob sank wearily into a hollow among the boulders. He lay back and wept as the sky darkened.

So much for the scheme to snatch the inheritance from my brother, he said to himself. Here I am, travelling alone, in the hope of finding refuge among my mother's relatives. Who knows if my brother isn't already on my trail, seeking to find me and kill me.

He watched as a star on the eastern horizon fluttered into brightness. "That is the direction in which I must travel," he said.

Tiredness overcame him, and he lay down to sleep with a stone for a pillow.

As he slept, he had a dream, and in that dream he saw a stairway reaching from the earth to heaven. Angels were going up and coming down on it. Then he saw the Lord standing beside him, speaking to him: "I am the Lord, the God of Abraham and Isaac. I will give to you and to your descendants this land on which you are lying . . . through you and your descendants I will bless all the nations."

The next morning when Jacob awoke, he took the stone that had been under his head and set it upright. "This stone will be a memorial to God," he said. And then he made a promise to God: "If you will be with me and protect me on this journey, and if you will provide for me the food and clothing that I need, and if I return safely to my father's home, then you will be my God."

Jacob and the Trickster

Jacob eventually arrived at the home of Laban, who was his mother's brother. He wept for joy when he realized his travels were over.

He was even more delighted to discover that Laban had two daughters. One, named Rachel, was very beautiful. Jacob asked to marry her.

"Work for me for seven years," said Laban, "and then she can be your wife."

So Jacob worked hard looking after his uncle's flocks, and with care and diligence helped to build the family's prosperity. When the time was up, he asked Laban to organize the wedding.

The bride was brought to the ceremony. The traditional clothes and heavy veil she wore were richly decorated and Jacob congratulated himself—he was marrying the lovely daughter of a wealthy man. That night, Jacob took the young woman for his wife.

The next day dawned. Jacob turned to see his wife in the clear morning light. He gasped in disbelief. "What are you doing here?" he hissed at the woman in his bed. He shook her angrily.

"It was my father's plan," she sobbed. "I had to do as he said." Jacob still swore at her. He had spent his wedding night with Rachel's sister, Leah. Laban had tricked him.

Then he set out to confront his uncle. When he saw Laban's knowing smile, his anger turned to noisy rage, like a flickering fire exploding into flame. He shouted, he cursed, he threatened.

"Be calm," said Laban. "It is simply not the custom here for the younger sister to marry before the elder. Agree to give me seven more years of your hard work and you can marry Rachel as soon as the celebrations for your marriage to Leah are over."

A group of muscular servants came and stood around Laban. Jacob fell silent. He could see he had no choice. He married Rachel as soon as he could, and, outwardly calm, he continued to work for Laban.

The flocks prospered under his care. Laban and Jacob appeared to be reconciled, especially when children were born and Laban found great delight in being a grandfather. Jacob saw his chance.

"Look at the fine animals in your flocks," he said. "See how they have multiplied. And yet, here and there, see a speckled sheep, and a dark-fleeced animal, one with ugly patches of cream and brown. Now I am the father of your grandchildren, perhaps you would allow me to build my flocks from these lesser specimens." Laban nodded his agreement.

But Jacob had not forgiven Laban his treachery. He bred the flocks in such a way that there were many spotted and speckled young, and so he grew rich.

Soon Laban's sons noticed what was happening, and Jacob and Laban argued bitterly. "You are stealing wealth from my sons," he stormed. Jacob decided to make his escape, but Laban caught up with him. "You have not even let me kiss my grandchildren good-bye," he pleaded.

The two tricksters eyed each other suspiciously. Finally, they reached an agreement. And Jacob set out to return to the land of Canaan where he had been born.

Jacob and Esau

Jacob had left Canaan as a fugitive, carrying nothing with him but a stick to lean on as he walked. He returned with a great household—his wives, his children, and his slaves; his cattle, his donkeys, and his flocks of sheep and goats. He knew that he was moving close to where his brother lived, and he was afraid.

Word reached him that Esau was approaching, bringing with him four hundred fighting men. Jacob's heart sank. "Deep inside, I knew that my brother would always remember the wrong I did him," he said. Quickly, Jacob divided his household into two groups. "If we are attacked, perhaps one of the groups will escape," he said.

He also selected livestock that he could give to his brother: goats and sheep, camels and cattle and donkeys. Perhaps I will win him over with these gifts, he said to himself. Perhaps he will forgive me what I did to him when I was young.

The night before he was to meet Esau, Jacob waited up alone. A mysterious stranger came and fought with him. They wrestled till just before daybreak, and the stranger saw he could not win. In a sudden move, the man struck Jacob on the hip, putting it out of joint. "Let me go," the man said. "Daylight is coming."

"I will not let you go unless you bless me," retorted Jacob.

"Tell me your name," said the stranger, and Jacob did.

"Your name will no longer be Jacob," he said. "You have struggled with God and with men and you have won, so your name will now be Israel."

"And what is your name?" asked Jacob. The stranger would not tell him, but he blessed Jacob and left.

Then Jacob who was called Israel realized who the stranger was—he had met God face to face.

Morning came and Jacob found he still walked with a limp. In many ways I am strong, he reflected, but with this injury, God has shown me that I am also frail. He walked slowly, painfully, and humbly toward Esau. As he drew near his brother, he bowed low.

Suddenly, he heard a great shout of laughter. Esau ran to greet him. He threw his arms around his younger brother and kissed him. He looked behind to the army of men he had gathered from his household. He looked beyond to the flocks that were his brother's. Then he laughed another hearty laugh. "Let the past be," he said, "and let us be glad for the future." The brothers who had parted as enemies agreed to live side by side as friends.

The Story of Joseph

Jacob's new name of Israel occurs time and again throughout the Bible.
His twelve sons each had families, and over many generations they become
known as the twelve tribes of Israel—the people of Israel.

❦

Jacob had twelve sons: to his wife Leah had been born Reuben, Simeon, Levi, Judah, Issachar, and Zebulun. Her slave had borne him Gad and Asher. Rachel's slave had borne him Dan and Naphtali.

The sons Jacob loved most were those who had been born of his cherished wife, Rachel. They were the youngest, and their names were Joseph and Benjamin.

Jacob let everyone see that, for him, Joseph was the most important of his sons, and he gave him a beautifully decorated robe. The very sight of Joseph wearing it made the other brothers jealous and they would not even speak to him.

But Joseph still spoke to them. He even sought them out and spoke boastfully. "Listen to my dream," he said one day. "We were all in the field tying up sheaves of wheat. My sheaf stood up tall. Yours gathered around it and bowed down to it. What do you think of that?"

"Do you think you're going to lord it over us?" they sneered. And they hated him all the more.

Then Joseph had another dream. "Listen to this," he said. "In my dream I saw the sun and the moon and eleven stars bowing down to me." He told his father of this dream, and even Jacob was angry.

"Do you think that your mother and your brothers and I are going to bow down to you?" he scolded.

The whole family grew suspicious of Joseph.

"He dreams too much of power," said his brothers.

"Yet I have so much wanted Joseph to have all the wealth and acclaim I longed for as a young man," said Jacob, as he brushed a trace of mud off the expensive robe he had bought his son.

Joseph just smiled.

Joseph Is Sold

One day, Joseph's brothers were out taking care of their father's flock. Jacob sent Joseph to visit them. "Make sure that all is well with them," he said, "and then come back and tell me."

When the brothers saw him approaching, they began to grumble.

"Is that the high and mighty Prince Joseph?" called one.

"In his dreams!" mocked the rest.

"Let's kill him and throw his body down a well," they said. "We can say that a wild animal killed him."

Only Reuben hesitated. "Let's just throw him down a well and leave him out here in the wilderness," he said. That way, he thought, as he set out with the flocks, I can come and rescue him and send him on his way home.

The others agreed to Reuben's plan. When Joseph came up, they ripped the beautiful robe off his back and threw him into a dry well. "Ha!" they laughed. "Are the sun, moon, and stars bowing down to Joseph down there? Is his dream coming true?"

While they were eating and laughing, they saw a caravan of camels and foreign traders crossing the wilderness with spices and precious goods to be sold in the markets of Egypt far to the south.

Judah spoke up. "Let's sell Joseph as a slave," he said. "Then we will be rid of him, but we will not have murdered our own brother."

Joseph was pulled out of the well and handed over in exchange for twenty pieces of silver.

Reuben returned and found that the well was empty. He was distraught. "Our brother is gone!" he cried. Even when he heard what had happened, he was still inconsolable. "What will we tell our father?" he lamented.

The brothers decided to make Joseph's disappearance look like a terrible accident. They killed one of the flock and dipped the torn pieces of Joseph's robe in the blood. They took it back to Jacob. "We found this," they said. "Do you recognize it?"

Jacob knew all too well what it was and believed his son had been torn to pieces by a wild animal.

"My son, my own dear son," he wept.

Joseph the Slave

While Jacob was grieving for the son he believed was dead, Joseph was sold to a wealthy Egyptian named Potiphar, the captain of the pharaoh's palace guard. Joseph became a lowly slave, but God was taking care of him. Potiphar noticed that Joseph was a good worker and soon put him in charge of his household.

Joseph was a handsome young man now, and Potiphar's wife was delighted.

That young man is much more attractive than my dull old Potiphar, she said to herself, and an idea took root in her mind. One afternoon, she had her room prepared as a love nest and invited Joseph to join her in bed.

"That would be wrong and . . . I am your husband's loyal servant," mumbled Joseph, feeling deeply embarrassed. "Come on," she urged, tugging at his clothes. Joseph struggled to escape and ran off, but part of his clothing was torn away.

Potiphar's wife looked at the garment in her hand. She felt insulted and humiliated. As soon as her husband returned she rushed to speak to him, waving the piece of cloth. "That young Joseph marched right into my room when I was practically *naked*," she wailed, "and no one came when I screamed because he had sent them to do jobs too far away to hear. If I hadn't fought him off with my nails . . ."

Potiphar had heard enough. He had Joseph thrown into jail.

The Egyptian cell was darker than any pit in the wilderness. Yet God was still with him, and Joseph remained as dutiful as ever. When two other prisoners arrived, and Joseph was made their servant, he made up his mind to do the job well.

The men had both been important officials: the pharaoh's wine steward and the pharaoh's baker. One morning, when they awoke, each was puzzled by a dream.

"God has given me the ability to interpret dreams," said Joseph. "Tell me what you saw."

The wine steward spoke first. "I dreamed of a grapevine with three branches," he said. "It came into leaf, and then the blossoms appeared, and almost at once the fruit grew and ripened. I had the pharaoh's cup in my hand, so I squeezed the grapes and took the wine to him."

"This is what your dream means," said Joseph. "In three days, you will be released from prison and you will be made the pharaoh's wine steward once more. Remember me when you are free."

Then the baker spoke: "I dreamed I was carrying three baskets on my head. Inside were pastries for the pharaoh, but the birds were eating them."

"This is what your dream means," said Joseph. "In three days you will be released from prison . . . but only because the pharaoh wants to have your head cut off. He will hang your body where the birds can eat it."

The two men looked at him—one with hope, the other with dread. "Meanwhile," said Joseph, "I will serve you both as best I can."

Everything happened just as Joseph had said. However, the wine steward forgot all about Joseph once he was back in the pharaoh's service. It seemed that the young man would stay in prison forever.

Joseph and the Pharaoh

Two years passed after Joseph had told the wine steward the meaning of his dream. The man was enjoying a comfortable life as the highly respected servant of the pharaoh and was among the first to know when, one morning, the pharaoh awoke, troubled by a dream.

The court magicians were quickly summoned to see if they could explain it.

"I was standing by the River Nile," said the pharaoh. "Seven fat cows came out of the river and they began to eat the grass. Then seven thin cows came out of the river and they ate the fat cows. I woke up, puzzled. Then I fell asleep again. I saw seven plump ears of grain. Then seven more ears sprouted, but a hot wind blew in from the wilderness and they dried up and were empty. They swallowed up the ears that were full."

"Strange," said the chief magician.

"Very odd," said another magician.

"Utterly puzzling," chorused the rest.

As none of the magicians knew what to make of the dream, and the pharaoh was growing angry, the wine steward spoke up. "You will remember, O Pharaoh, that you were angry with the chief baker and me a couple of years ago. In jail we were given a young slave to be our servant. He told us the meaning of our dreams, and things turned out just as he said."

The pharaoh sent for Joseph. "I hear you can interpret dreams," he said.

"I cannot do so myself," replied Joseph, "but God will show me the meaning." So the pharaoh told his dreams again and Joseph listened carefully.

"The two dreams mean the same thing," he said. "Soon there will be seven years of plenty, with abundant harvests. Then there will follow seven years of famine, and the lean years will eat up all the good things the country had in the prosperous years. So this is what you must do. Choose a man who is wise and has good judgment, and put him in charge of the country. Arrange for a portion of the harvests in the next seven years to be put into storage. Then you will have enough to feed your people during the famine."

The pharaoh was very impressed and put Joseph in charge at once. He gave him a fine linen robe, the ring with the royal seal from his own finger, a gold chain to wear around his neck, and the second royal chariot to ride in. Joseph travelled around the country making sure his orders were carried out, and a guard went ahead of him, crying, "Make way!"

And so, in each city of Egypt, great storehouses were filled with grain for the years of hardship to come.

Joseph Meets His Brothers

The years of famine came, just as Joseph had said. Crops failed throughout Egypt, and in the lands beyond. In Canaan, Joseph's family feared starvation.

The news spread that, for a price, grain could be bought in Egypt. "The pharaoh has found an excellent man to guide his country through the famine," travellers reported. "This man had the foresight to insist on storing grain over seven years of good harvests. Now, he is overseeing the distribution of grain through the lean years. He will grant an audience to those who wish to appeal to him."

Jacob gathered his sons around him. "We are all feeling the pain of this devastating famine," he said. "It seems our only hope is to go to appeal to this governor of Egypt. I know the distance is great, but I want you all to go together and ask to buy food for the family . . . all except my precious Benjamin, who is too young."

The journey took the brothers through the dusty wilderness—a bleak landscape of rock and sand and thorn bushes. They arrived, worn out and in tattered robes, and were brought before the stern-faced governor in his gleaming robes and glittering jewels. They bowed low before him, their faces to the ground.

Joseph recognized them at once, but he did not say so. Instead he spoke harshly in Egyptian, and an interpreter spoke between them.

"You are spies, aren't you?" he said. "You have come to find out where our country is weak."

"No indeed," they replied. "We come from a family of twelve brothers. One brother is dead, and the youngest is with our father in the land of Canaan."

"I don't believe you," replied Joseph. "Can you tell me the exact story of how your brother died?"

The brothers bit their lips and Joseph laughed at their consternation. Then he spoke again: "I'm more interested in the brother you say has stayed in Canaan. I want to put what you say to the test. One of you will stay here as a hostage. Go back to your family with a supply of grain, and then return with the young brother you speak of."

"You see what has happened," said Reuben to his brothers. "We are being paid back for what we did to Joseph."

Joseph could understand every word they said, and when he heard this, he had to leave the room to hide his tears. When he could speak again, he returned and had Simeon thrown into jail. The others he sent back to Canaan.

Joseph and Benjamin

Jacob ran to greet his sons when they returned from Egypt. "So you have succeeded!" he cried in delight.

"In part," said Reuben. "We have full sacks, Father, but we were suspected of spying, and Simeon has been kept as a hostage. Worse than that, as we travelled, we found the money we paid lying on top of the grain. If we return, we could be accused of stealing. If we do not return, then Simeon will never go free."

Jacob looked at his sons with anguish clouding his eyes, and his face seemed to turn ashen.

"If we do go back," continued Reuben, "then we must take Benjamin. That was part of the arrangement."

Jacob was silent for a long time. "I will not let him go," he said. "I have already lost Joseph."

Time passed and the famine grew even more severe.

"Very well," Jacob agreed at last. "Take honey and spices and nuts with you as gifts, and twice as much money as you need to buy grain, so you can pay for what was in your sacks last time. Take Benjamin . . . but return at once. Maybe God will cause the Egyptian to take pity on us."

They went as instructed and were brought to Joseph. He invited them to eat with him, and as they ate, Joseph looked at his younger brother. Tears came to his eyes, and he had to leave the room. He returned and made sure that his guests had plenty of food and drink.

Before they left, he arranged for grain to be loaded into their packs, but he asked for his own silver cup to be put in Benjamin's sack secretly. Then he sent his brothers on their way home.

After they had gone a short distance, Joseph sent his servants after them. "Stop those men!" he said. "Ask them why they have been so wicked as to steal my cup when I have treated them so well."

When the brothers heard the accusation, they were dismayed. "If one of us has been dishonest, then let the thief be put to death," they agreed. "And the rest of us will be your slaves."

The cup was found in Benjamin's sack. Grim-faced, the Egyptian servants herded the family back to Joseph. Benjamin clung to Reuben, sobbing.

"The one who stole my cup must stay as my slave," Joseph declared. "The rest of you can go."

At this, Judah spoke up. "Let me stay instead," he pleaded. "If Benjamin does not return, our father will die of sorrow."

Joseph ordered his servants to leave the room, and then he broke down in tears.

"I am your brother Joseph," he wept. "It was God who sent me here ahead of you so I could rescue my family in this time of trouble," he said. "Now go, and fetch all the family. I will arrange with the pharaoh for you to be given land, so you can make your home here."

And so it was.

The Great Exodus

At Joseph's invitation, the sons of Israel made their home in Egypt, taking their households with them. Generations passed, and the families prospered. All seemed to be well, until a new pharoah came to the throne.

The pharaoh laid down his wine cup and gazed out of his pavilion. The landscape was bare and uninviting, but in the pharaoh's imagination, there arose a city more splendid than any other.

"We'll need a number of slaves, of course," said the man at his side. He was the architect who had brought the pharaoh the plans for the building scheme, and there was a trace of anxiety in his voice. "But, of course, Your Majesty can have anything he desires."

The pharaoh smiled. "I can," he said. "But it is useful to have the support of the people."

Soon afterward, the pharaoh took his plan to his subjects. "There are too many of those foreigners dwelling among us," he said to them. "If we went to war against another nation, we could not trust them to fight with us. They might turn on us and take control of the land . . . *our* land. We must find a way to stop them from becoming too numerous and too powerful."

The Egyptians caught his mood. "Let us make them our slaves," it was agreed. "Let us make them work to build our cities. Let us wear the Israelites out with toil while we grow richer and enjoy a life of leisure."

So it was that some Egyptians were appointed to be slave drivers: brutal and violent men who took delight in being cruel and who whipped the Israelites to make them work harder.

But the people of Israel continued to grow in number. The pharaoh remained worried. He spoke to the two midwives who helped the Israelite women when they gave birth.

"When you deliver a baby girl," he said, "you may let her live, but whenever an Israelite boy is born, make sure that he dies. . . ." He gave the women a sideways, menacing glance.

The midwives feared God more than the pharaoh. "We can't get to the women in time to do as you say," they lied. "Israelite women give birth easily, with no complications. The babies are crying noisily before we ever get near them."

"Then I have another plan," said the pharaoh. "This one will not fail. Take every newborn Israelite boy," he ordered his people, "and throw each one into the River Nile."

The Baby Moses

In a low, mud-brick house, an Israelite woman whispered a secret to her two children as she put them to bed.

"Another baby!" said the boy. "I hope it's a boy—someone for me to play with!"

"Don't be silly, Aaron, we must hope it's a girl," said the daughter, Miriam, "then the pharaoh's soldiers won't come and drown it." Her eyes filled with tears. "Mother, what will we do if it's a boy?"

"We will hide him," she explained to her children. "We will all work together to keep him safe."

So they did, for the baby was a boy. But when the child was three months old, they knew they could not hide him in their home any longer. "I have an idea," said the mother. "It is very risky, but we must try. Aaron, go down to the river and collect the kind of reeds I use for making a basket. Miriam, sit with me and learn how to coil them together."

All the family worked together to make a cradle-shaped basket with a matching lid. Aaron helped daub the outside with sticky tar. "Now not one drop of water will get in," he said proudly.

They set off as a little group, each carrying a basket, as if they were taking bread to a friend's house . . . and on the way, they slipped the cradle basket among the tall reeds that grew in a quiet eddy of the Nile. Miriam stayed close by. All was quiet, but for the occasional quack of a waterbird.

Then came a peal of laughter, and Miriam froze. "Oh!" she gasped. She could see a procession of Egyptian maidservants walking her way, and in the middle of the group was the pharaoh's own daughter, coming to the river to bathe.

The princess waded toward the pool where Miriam waited. "Here's a lovely sheltered place," she exclaimed. "Oh, there's something in the reeds. What's that, I wonder?"

A maidservant splashed forward and brought out the basket. She lifted the lid.

"Oh, it's a baby," the princess exclaimed. "It's a little Israelite, and the poor darling is crying. Oh, hush, little one, don't be upset." She looked around. "If this baby has been abandoned, I could be a mother to him. I could hire a nurse to feed him, and then bring him up myself."

Miriam crept forward. "Do you need someone to nurse the baby for you, ma'am?" she asked bravely.

The princess smiled. "Yes, please, if you know someone," she replied.

Miriam ran home. "Mother, come now, come now!" she cried. "The princess of Egypt wants someone to nurse the baby she's found—and it's our baby!"

Miriam's mother came, and found the princess cooing to her child. The slave girls had garlanded the cradle boat with flowers. As she approached, the princess held out the baby. "Please look after this child for me until he is old enough to come to the palace," she requested. And the child was given the name of Moses, a word meaning "pulled out," for he had been pulled out of the water.

Moses and His People

Moses became the adopted son of the Egyptian princess, and he grew up in the royal palace. When he was a young man, he went out to tour the places where his own people lived.

Why has no one told me what to expect? he wondered. The settlements were ramshackle, the children painfully thin, the adults gaunt with work and worry. Smug slave drivers wandered around the work camps, striking out viciously and at random.

"Get up, you good-for-nothing scum." One of the slave drivers had come across an Israelite sitting down wearily with his shovel a little apart from the work gang.

"Scum yourself," replied the Israelite bitterly.

Crack!

A whip slashed across him. Blinded with pain and rage the Israelite stood up and swung a fist at his tormentor. Blow followed blow . . . but the slave driver was too much of a match for the slave and, within a minute, the slave fell.

The slave driver would not stop. Moses was frozen in horror as the man kicked and whipped the slave in a mounting frenzy of violence.

Moses looked around to make sure no one was watching him. Then he took a step forward and struck out.

The Egyptian fell. His head cracked against a stone. He moaned a little, then slumped to the ground.

Moses shuddered. He had killed a man. He grabbed the shovel that the slave had been holding and scooped a shallow grave in the sand. Then he buried the slave driver as fast as he could and kicked stones over the place where he lay.

Moses struggled to put the horror of the day behind him. The following morning, he returned to the same place and found two Israelites fighting.

"Why are you beating up a fellow Israelite?" he demanded. "Is there not enough violence in your life?"

"Mind your own business," said one of the men. "Or are you going to kill me like you killed the Egyptian?" He winked slyly.

Moses was alarmed that people knew what had happened. He fled, fearful that the pharaoh would have him killed for his crime.

Moses and the Burning Bush

Moses left behind the fertile fields of Egypt close to the River Nile. He escaped to the barren wilderness to the east.

In that region lived a nomadic people known as the Midianites. Moses was made welcome among them. He married a Midianite woman and exchanged his rich life as prince in Egypt for the everyday toil of a wandering shepherd.

One day, he was leading his family's flocks of sheep and goats past the rocky Mount Sinai. The sun glared down on the bleached earth dotted with scrubby trees. Suddenly, he saw flames flickering out from a thorny bush. He blinked and looked harder. The bush was on fire, yet it was not being burned! As he drew closer he heard a voice.

"Moses! Moses!"

"Yes," he answered. "Here I am."

"Take off your sandals," said the voice. "You are standing on holy ground. I am the God of your ancestors, the God of Abraham and Isaac and Jacob."

Moses did as he was instructed. He listened as God told him of the suffering of his people in the land of Egypt. He listened as God told him that he, Moses, must go to the pharaoh and tell him to let the Israelites go to a new land.

"How . . . how can I do that?" asked Moses. "Years have passed since I was in Egypt. There is a new pharaoh. I am no one of importance now."

"I will be with you," replied God.

"And the Israelites," said Moses. "When I say that the God of their ancestors has sent me, they will ask me, 'What is the name of that God?' "

God said, "I am who I am. This what you must say to them: 'The one who is called "I AM" has sent me to you. . . . This is my name forever; this is what all future generations are to call me.' "

Then God gave Moses the power to work miracles. When he threw down his staff, it became a snake. When he picked it up, it became a staff again. With such wonders, he could prove that he was indeed sent by God.

But Moses was still hesitant. "I've always stumbled over my words," he said. "I'm such a poor speaker that people don't listen to me."

God reassured him. "I will help you speak. Now go!"

When Moses hesitated yet again, God became impatient and said, "Take your brother, Aaron, with you. You can make him do all the talking—he is good at it. You will be like God, telling him what to say. And I will work miracles and wonders for you so that the pharaoh will let you go."

Moses Goes to the Pharaoh

Moses led his flocks back to where his family was camped. He asked his father-in-law for permission to leave the animals and to travel back to Egypt to visit his people. Then he set out with his wife and his children.

On the way, he met Aaron, as God had promised. Moses told his brother of all that had happened and of how God had said that they should work together to arrange for the Israelites to go free.

The two men presented themselves at the Egyptian court.

"What nonsense is this?" mocked the pharaoh. "You can't expect me to let my slaves go. In fact . . . I think the Israelites should work harder!" He was so angry that he changed the orders for the slave drivers. Previously, the Israelites had been given straw to strengthen the mud bricks they made. Now they had to find their own straw . . . and still make as many bricks.

The slaves complained bitterly. When they found out that Moses and Aaron had made the pharaoh angry, they turned against the two men. Moses, in turn, complained to God.

"I am the Lord," said God. "You must tell the Israelites that I am their God and that I will set them free."

"But . . . they don't listen," protested Moses.

"And tell the pharaoh that he must let them go," said God.

Reluctantly, the two men returned to the pharaoh with their request. Aaron showed the pharaoh and his men a miracle to prove that God was with him. He threw his stick down, and it became a snake. He picked it up, and it became a stick again.

Then the court magicians performed the same wonder.

"See," said the pharaoh, "you are not doing anything special."

Then Aaron's stick swallowed up the sticks belonging to the court magicians.

But the pharaoh was unmoved. "Get out of my sight!" he said. "The Israelites stay in Egypt as my slaves."

The Stubborn Pharaoh

Moses was dismayed. He firmly believed that God had told him to lead his people to freedom, but the pharaoh was not willing to let them go.

Then God spoke to him again: "The pharaoh is very stubborn. Tomorrow, meet him when he walks down to the Nile. Ask him again to let the Israelites go free. If he refuses, lift the stick that was turned into a snake and strike the water. It will turn to blood."

Moses and Aaron did as God said, and the water turned red and began to stink horribly. But then the court magicians showed they could work the same wonder by magic. The pharaoh would not change his mind.

Next, God told Moses to warn the pharaoh that there would be a great horde of frogs all over the land of Egypt if he would not let the people go. Yet again, the pharaoh refused. So the frogs came hopping and jumping. They jumped up on people's beds and crouched in among the baking pans. But the magicians showed that they, too, could make frogs appear, and the pharaoh would not change his mind.

Then came other disasters. First came a swarm of gnats . . . and this time, the magicians could not work the same wonder. Next came great clouds of flies. After that, a terrible disease came upon all the animals that the Egyptians owned, and the animals died. The pharaoh still refused to let the Israelites leave the land.

After that came an epidemic of a skin disease that caused open sores and painful boils. The pharaoh remained unmoved at the suffering among his own people. Moses warned him of another disaster: a storm of hail that would destroy all the crops. In the midst of the storm, the pharaoh admitted he was wrong, and he begged Moses to pray to his God for the hail to stop.

But when all was calm, he changed his mind.

"Do not worry," said God. "In years to come, people will tell of these disasters and know that your God is powerful." So Moses went again to the pharaoh and warned him that locusts would invade the land if he did not let the people go.

The locusts came and ate everything that the hail had left. Again the pharaoh begged Moses to ask God to send them away but, once they had gone, he still refused to let the people go.

Then darkness fell upon the land. "Your people may go to worship God in the wilderness," he said, "but your animals must stay here."

"No, that is not what I am asking for," replied Moses.

"Then I won't change my mind at all," said the pharaoh. "Now get out of my sight!"

The Passover

It seemed that nothing would persuade the pharaoh to let the Israelites go. Then God spoke to Moses again. "A worse punishment than anything that has gone before is going to fall on the Egyptians," God warned.

Moses and Aaron returned to the pharaoh to tell him. "Let my people go," said Moses. "If you do not, then one night, at midnight, every firstborn son will die."

The pharaoh appeared not to notice. He was playing with a kitten, dangling a ball on a piece of string in front of the little creature and whisking it away when the kitten pounced.

Finally, he looked up. But it was to his servants that he spoke: "These men are always wasting my time! Take them away!"

Moses and Aaron returned to the Israelites. God had given clear instructions about what the people had to do. On a certain day, they were to prepare a special meal. Each household was to take a lamb, kill it, and roast it. Some of its blood was to be used to mark a sign around the door of their home so that the Angel of Death would see it and pass over the house. The meat was to be served with bitter salad herbs and bread made quickly without any yeast.

At midnight of the appointed day, as God had said, a great weeping and wailing was heard all over the land, for in every Egyptian home the firstborn son lay dead, but the angel had passed over the Israelite dwellings.

"Go, get out, leave us in peace!" cried the Egyptians. "Take what you want and go elsewhere!"

"We still have bread to bake," protested the Israelite women.

"Take it with you," urged the Egyptians. "Just put it in a pan and carry it. We don't want you anymore."

Even the pharaoh wanted the Israelites to go now.

And so Moses finally led his people out of Egypt. It was the start of a journey to the land of Canaan, the place where Abraham had dreamed his descendants would make their home.

Moses said to the people, "Remember this day—the day on which you left Egypt, the place where you were slaves. The Lord has solemnly promised to give you the land of Canaan. When he brings you into that rich and fertile land, you must celebrate this Passover festival in the first month of every year. When the festival begins, explain to your children that you do all this because of what the Lord did for you when you left Egypt."

70

Crossing the Red Sea

The people of Israel were a huge, jostling throng, with their flocks of sheep and goats and cattle. As they travelled, they saw before them a pillar of cloud in the daytime, and at night a pillar of fire. "See!" they said. "The Lord is leading us."

They were led in a roundabout route to the shore of the Red Sea, where they made their camp.

However, back in Egypt, the pharaoh heard of their escape.

"What have we done? The Israelites were our slaves and we have lost them!" He was roused to a frenzy of action.

"Quick! Assemble the army, and its finest chariots and charioteers. Let us go and force those troublesome people to return to the slave camps."

When the Israelites saw the army, they were terrified. At once they began to blame Moses. "See! Your so-called bid for freedom has failed. Now we will die here in the desert. It would have been better if we had stayed in Egypt as slaves."

"Don't be afraid," replied Moses. "I have often felt discouraged myself. But through the hard times, I have seen more clearly how great is God's power to help us and defend us. Just watch what happens today."

Then God told Moses to raise his stick and hold it out over the water of the Red Sea. A strong wind began to blow, and the waters divided so that the people could walk on dry ground, with walls of water on either side.

The Egyptians pursued them at a furious pace. But the ground under the chariot wheels grew soft and the wheels became stuck. The drivers looked in alarm at the water on either side.

On the far shore, Moses lifted his hand over the sea again. The sea rolled in over the pathway. The Egyptian army was destroyed.

Moses and all the people celebrated their escape and were amazed at the power of the God who had saved them.

"The Lord is my strong defender;
he is the one who has saved me."

Exodus 15:2

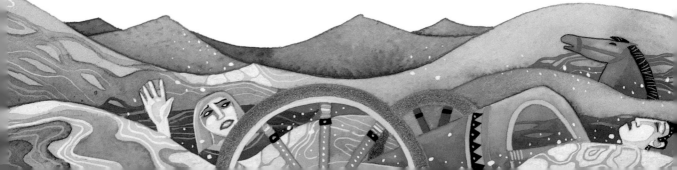

Wanderings in the Wilderness

The Israelites had escaped from slavery. To the northeast lay the land of Canaan,
a fertile land that they believed was the land promised to them by God. The wilderness
that stretched ahead of them would not take long to cross. The plan was to enter the
new land and make it their own . . . but when they saw that the cities of Canaan
were strongly defended, they chose to stay as nomads in the desert.

Moses led the people of Israel out into the wilderness beyond the Red Sea.
Water was hard to find. At last, they came to a place where there was a
pool of water. Eagerly they reached for it, only to find that it was bitter. The
people began to complain again.

"What are we going to drink?" they lamented.

Moses prayed to God for help. While he was praying, he saw a piece of wood.
At once he knew that he must throw this wood into the water. When he did so,
by a miracle, the bitter water became fit to drink.

Next, food became scarce. "We were better off in Egypt," the people
complained. "At least there we had enough to eat. Here, we are going to die of
starvation."

But God spoke to Moses: "I am going to make food rain down from the sky."
The whole nation saw the dazzling light of God's presence, and they waited to
see what would happen next.

In the evening, a flock of quails flew in, and the people were able to catch
them to eat as food. In the morning, the people awoke to find dew all around.
When it dried in the heat of the sun, they found silvery flakes left on every
surface. These they gathered, and they discovered it was food that tasted like
wafers made with honey. They called this food "manna."

In ways like these, God provided for the people.

> Some wandered in the trackless desert
>   and could not find their way to a city to live in.
> They were hungry and thirsty
>   and had given up all hope.
> Then in their trouble they called to the Lord,
>   and he saved them from their distress.

Psalm 107:4–6

The Great Commandments

At last, the people came to Mount Sinai. Moses walked up the rock-strewn slopes where, in the stillness, he believed he would hear the voice of God.

"Here is my message for the Israelites," God said. "Say to them, 'See I have brought you safely out of Egypt, as an eagle carries young on its wings. If you obey me, and live in agreement with me, then you will be my special people.' "

Moses told them what God had said, and he also told them to prepare to worship God from the foot of the mountain. On the appointed day, there came thunder and lightning, and a thick cloud engulfed the mountaintop. Then came the sound of a trumpet blast. Flames darted from the rocky peaks and smoke billowed down to the plain. The people trembled with fear.

God called to Moses and told him that the people must stay on the plain below, and only Moses could cross the boundary onto the sacred mountain. Then God gave these commandments to Moses:

"I am the Lord your God, who brought you out of Egypt where you were slaves. Worship no god but me.

"Do not make for yourselves images of anything in heaven or on earth or in the water under the earth. Do not bow down to any idol or worship it, because I am the Lord your God and I tolerate no rivals. I bring punishment on those who hate me and on their descendants down to the third and fourth generation. But I show my love to thousands of generations of those who love me and obey my laws.

"Do not use my name for evil purposes, for I, the Lord your God, will punish anyone who misuses my name.

"Observe the Sabbath and keep it holy. You have six days in which to do your work, but the seventh day is a day of rest dedicated to me. On that day, no one is to work—neither you, your children, your slaves, your animals, nor the foreigners who live in your country. In six days I, the Lord, made the earth, the sky, the sea, and everything in them, but on the seventh day I rested. That is why I, the Lord, blessed the Sabbath and made it holy.

"Respect your father and your mother, so that you may live a long time in the land that I am giving you.

"Do not commit murder.

"Do not commit adultery.

"Do not steal.

"Do not accuse anyone falsely.

"Do not desire another man's house; do not desire his wife, his slaves, his cattle, his donkeys, or anything else that he owns."

Obedience and Disobedience

God gave the people many instructions to guide them: laws that would lead them in the ways of justice and fairness. They were to treat their own people honestly and deal kindly with any who struggled to make a living among them—the poor, the foreigners, the orphans.

In a solemn ceremony, the leaders of the Israelites agreed to live as God's people.

Then God told Moses to meet with him on top of Mount Sinai; there God would give him two stone tablets on which the laws would be engraved forever. Moses set off and left Aaron in charge of the people below.

Moses was gone for many days and the people grew tired of waiting. They complained to Aaron, "Moses has gone, and we have no one to lead us. Let us make our own god."

The agreement they had made with God was abandoned. They took their gold finery and melted it down so it could be poured into a cast, and in this way they made for themselves a golden bull. "This is our god," they cried, and they organized a festival of worship.

The dancing and clapping began, and young women played tambourines while men played joyful melodies on pipes.

"It's not really a party for us," the children muttered, and they hid under tables as the dancing grew wilder and the grown-ups drank more than they should.

"It's horrible to think what's going on," they whispered from under their blankets, trying to shut out the rowdiness and mayhem that shattered the night.

God and God's laws had been forgotten.

Moses came down from the mountain. He saw what the people were doing, and he was furious at their disobedience. He smashed the stone tablets he was carrying, and the scattered fragments showed how the agreement with God was destroyed. Then he seized the golden bull and melted it down. He called for those who were on the Lord's side to come forward, and he set them against those who still had no regard for God.

Then he went back to God, to pray that God would forgive the people.

God told Moses to cut two stone tablets like the first ones, and said that the agreement with the people could be renewed. God said this: "I, the Lord, am a God who is full of compassion and pity, who is not easily angered and who shows great love and faithfulness. I keep my promise for thousands of generations and forgive evil and sin, but I will not fail to punish children and grandchildren to the third and fourth generation for the sins of their parents."

Then, as God instructed, the people set to work to make for themselves a tent of worship—a tabernacle. Its outer coverings of leather and canvas kept out the harsh winds of the wilderness. Inside was beauty and calm. Priests in white robes performed the ceremonies of sacrifice and worship amid embroidered hangings of red and blue, and cleverly crafted furniture of the finest gold. By the light that shone from seven lamps on a golden lampstand, the golden box was carried into the innermost part of the tent. It was the Ark of the Covenant—the box containing the record of the agreement between God and the people, an agreement God promised to respect forever.

The Death of Moses

For forty long years, the people of Israel travelled around the wilderness. In that time, Aaron died, and Moses grew to be an old man. He knew that the time was coming when the Israelites would enter the land of Canaan and make it their home. He was concerned that they should remember all God's laws and keep them faithfully. So he chose a man to be leader in his stead—a young soldier named Joshua. Then he addressed the people:

"These are all the laws that the Lord your God commanded me to teach you. Obey them in the land that you are about to enter and occupy. As long as you live, you and your descendants are to worship the Lord your God and obey all his laws that I am giving you, so that you may live in that land a long time. Listen to them, people of Israel, and obey them! Then all will go well with you, and you will become a mighty nation and live in that rich and fertile land, just as the Lord, the God of our ancestors, has promised.

"Israel, remember this! The Lord—and the Lord alone—is our God. Love the Lord your God with all your heart, with all your soul, and with all your strength. Never forget these commands that I am giving you today. Teach them to your children. Repeat them when you are at home and when you are away, when you are resting and when you are working. Tie them on your arms and wear them on your foreheads as a reminder. Write them on the doorposts of your houses and on your gates."

When Moses had finished all he had to say, God told him that the time had come for him to go and survey the future that lay before the nation.

"Climb Mount Nebo," said God. "From there you will be able to see all the lands where the Israelites will make their home."

He saw the hills to the north, paling in the hazy sunshine. He saw the mountains that ran the length of the country, shimmering blue in the distance, and knew that beyond them lay the lowlands that swept down to the sea. He saw the deep valley through which the River Jordan wound its majestic way to the Dead Sea. Beyond it was a wide plain, on which he could see the palm trees that marked the city of Jericho, famed for its springs of water.

Then, before his people entered Canaan, Moses died. In a place that no one ever found, his body lay down in its final resting place.

The Story of Joshua

After the death of Moses, Joshua took his appointed place as the new leader
of the people of Israel. It was his task to lead his people into Canaan . . .
the land the Israelites had refused to enter when they first saw it.

❦

Joshua sat looking into the distance. The landscape before his eyes shimmered
in the heat and the mist that rose up from the River Jordan in the valley
below. He was not so much looking as remembering—the time when Moses was
still alive, and he was one of the band of brave young soldiers sent out to survey
the land. It was the time of year when the grapes begin to ripen, and in the forty
days they had spent exploring, the fruit had turned from pale green to a deep,
luscious purple. He remembered the nights under the stars with his companions,
feasting on grapes they had not tended and laughing about the good wine they
would make when this land was theirs.

"That's it," they had said. "Let's find a huge bunch of grapes, and take that
back to the camp."

"Yes, that'll convince everyone," they had agreed. "We've had enough of
hanging around, wondering if we should move into Canaan, but our families
will need a reason to take on the challenge."

"Indeed, they will be scared to fight the tribes in Hebron. Did you ever see
people so tall? They must be descended from giants!"

"And we're going to need a clever strategy to take the cities. The walls are too
high to scale, and the gates are strongly made."

In the morning light, the young men had found the biggest bunch of grapes
they had ever seen. It was so large they had had to strap it to a pole so two men
could carry it between them. They had picked pomegranates and figs and
returned in a mood of great celebration.

Then, as they had stood before their people, their spirit of adventure had died. All except one of Joshua's companions, the faithful Caleb, had lost their nerve. "It's a fertile land," they had reported, "but too well defended. We could never make it our own."

"In fact," they had argued, "the harvest there isn't very good. The land has hardly produced enough for the people who live there now."

Joshua remembered his disbelief at the way his friends were behaving, his dismay at the decision of the people not to enter the land, and the disasters that had followed.

Now it was his turn to lead the people to that same land. For a moment, he wavered. Then came a new thought, a thought so loud he knew it must be God speaking to him: Joshua, no one will be able to defeat you as long as you live. I will always be with you; I will never abandon you. Obey the whole Law that my servant Moses gave you. Don't be afraid or discouraged, for I, the Lord your God, am with you wherever you go.

Spies

Joshua was filled with enthusiasm. He gathered the leaders of the different families of Israel together. "Let us all get ready," he said, "for in a matter of days we will move into Canaan."

He sent two men ahead to spy on the land.

"Go to Jericho," he said. "Find out what you can that will help us take the city, in spite of its mighty fortifications."

The men idled their way past the gatekeepers in the busy daytime. As evening fell, and the inhabitants of the city returned to their homes, they fell to wondering—where could they spend the night without being noticed?

"People are beginning to look at us," one whispered to the other. "That old man has had his eye on us for a while now."

"And that woman there, she's been gazing out of her window for ages. . . ."

As they looked up, the woman smiled. Then she smiled again.

"I get the strong impression that lady is asking us to spend the night at her place," grinned one of the spies.

So they went to the house of Rahab, a prostitute. Meanwhile, news about the strangers reached the king, and he sent an urgent message.

"Rahab," the messenger whispered, "the men in your house are Israelites. They have come to spy on our land. They plan to invade it. Bring them out— there are soldiers here to deal with them."

Rahab's smile was coy and charming. "There were two men who came here," she said, "but they left at sunset, before the city gate closed. They can't be far."

The king's men left in pursuit, and Rahab hurried to the roof of her home. She rummaged among the bundles of flax that were lying there to dry. "Wake up, wake up!" she whispered to the men she had hidden there. "I know your people are strong enough to capture our city. I've saved you from the king's men, and I can tell you where to hide in the hills so they do not find you. But when you return in battle, spare me and my family."

The men agreed and gave her a red cord to tie as a sign at her window when the battle came. Rahab's house was built into the city wall, and she let the men down to the ground outside. So they escaped to return to their people with their news.

Into Canaan

The day after the spies returned from Jericho with their report, Joshua ordered the people of Israel to strike camp.

"Today," he said, "we cross the River Jordan into the land of Canaan."

The priests went ahead, carrying with them the precious Ark of the Covenant, which contained the terms of the agreement between God and Israel.

It was the time of year when the Jordan is in flood, when the turbulent waters tumble down the valley, swirling over the banks and swallowing up rocks and bushes in their path.

Undaunted, the priests stepped into the river. As they did so, the waters stopped flowing and gathered into a great pool far upstream. The people of Israel walked into Canaan on dry land.

Then God told Joshua to command the priests to carry the Ark of the Covenant with them out of the river. When they reached the bank, the waters that had waited upstream surged forward with a great roar and plunged down the riverbed to the Dead Sea.

Israel, the Lord who created you says,
"Do not be afraid—I will save you.
 I have called you by name—you are mine.
When you pass through deep waters, I will be with you;
 your troubles will not overwhelm you."

Isaiah 43:1–2

The Battle of Jericho

The Israelites made their camp on the plain near Jericho. It was time to celebrate the Passover meal, the yearly reminder of God's leading them safely out of Egypt. The next day, they prepared their first meal from grain that had been grown in Canaan.

Meanwhile, the king of Jericho had ordered that the gates of his city be kept shut. Around the walls, his soldiers were on the alert, ready to hail arrows and stones on any attackers who might draw near.

From his vantage point, one Canaanite soldier saw a blur of activity near the Israelite camp. "What do you suppose that is?" he murmured. Other soldiers gathered to watch, grim and anxious, as a strange procession approached.

They heard an eerie wailing. At the head of the column were armed men, but following them were priests clad in white robes blowing a mournful, tuneless sound on ram's horn trumpets. Behind came more priests, carrying a box that was slung on poles. At the end came a long line of soldiers walking with a slow, deliberate tread.

The sentries on the walls gripped their weapons. The procession came close to the walls, then circled the entire city. Then it went away. There was no attack.

The same thing happened the next day, and the next . . . for six days.

By the seventh day, the guards on the city walls were less tense. "I suppose those wandering, beggar people think they are scaring us," they crowed, shaking their fists at them with amusement and disdain. Joshua's little army wore battered clothes, and the weapons they carried were simple and old-fashioned. But this time, the procession did not leave. It went around the city twice, three times.

Four times. Five times. Six times. (How much longer would this go on?) Seven times. Then a shout! A blast of trumpets! A great cry of triumph from all the army.

Suddenly, the masonry was crumbling under the feet of the guards. There were screams and shouts as the walls collapsed.

The Israelites marched in and took the city in a deadly attack. They found Rahab's house and brought her out to safety with her family. They searched for precious metals—gold and silver, bronze and iron to take as the spoils of battle, and they burned the city to the ground.

From that day on, Joshua led his people to victory in the land of Canaan. He divided the country into different territories and cities so that there was a home for each of the twelve families descended from Israel. When, after many years, the people were settled, he called their leaders to a solemn gathering. He reminded them of the faithfulness of the God who had guided them through the years.

"Now," said Joshua, "you must worship the Lord and serve your God sincerely and faithfully. Are you prepared to turn away from the gods that other nations worship? You must decide. As for me and my family, we will serve the Lord."

The people all agreed to do the same. Knowing that he had completed the task he had been given, Joshua died peacefully at the age of a hundred and ten.

The Stories of the Heroes

The people of Israel had promised Joshua they would be faithful to their God. After Joshua died, however, many of them were drawn to worshipping other gods. The Bible tells that when they turned their back on God, they were defeated by their enemies. When they repented, they prospered. Leading them to victory was a succession of great heroes, known as judges.

The people of Israel turned their back on God, and they forgot the laws of love and justice they had been given. So it was that God let the people of Midian rule over them. These were a fierce people of the desert—raiders and plunderers. They rode on camels and came swooping down on the Israelites, destroying their crops and stealing their flocks of animals. The people of Israel cried to God for help.

Why do we have to suffer in this way? wondered a young Israelite named Gideon. He was hard at work threshing grain within the walls of a tiny wine press, hoping that the Midianites would not see that he had grain worth stealing.

A stranger appeared. "The Lord is with you," was the stranger's greeting.

"How can you say that?" snorted Gideon. "If the Lord is with us, why are the Midianites tormenting us so? In days gone by, the Lord brought our people out of Egypt, where they were slaves. Now we are abandoned to our enemies."

"You go and rescue your people," came the reply. "I, the Lord, will help you, and you will crush them as easily as if they were just one man."

Gideon was unsure, but then the stranger miraculously called down fire. Gideon knew that the one speaking to him was God, and that he must do as the Lord commanded him.

"Your family has built an altar to the foreign god Baal," said the Lord to Gideon. "Your first task is to tear it down."

Now Gideon was very afraid. To tear down the altar was to tear down the very thing in which his people put their deepest trust. To destroy it would call forth fear and anger. He did as he was commanded, but secretly, when it was dark.

The whole community was enraged when they saw what had happened. They sought to find out who was to blame. "Bring us Gideon!" they shouted to his father. "He will pay for his action with his life."

"Let Baal defend himself," retorted Gideon's father. "It was his altar."

The so-called god remained silent and worked no wonders. Suddenly uncertain and insecure, the people stopped their shouting. With calm and determination, Gideon reestablished the worship of the God of Israel.

Gideon and the Midianites

The people of Israel reunited as faithful worshippers of their God. The enemies of Israel were afraid and met together: the Midianites, the Amalekites, and other tribes who lived in the wilderness beyond the River Jordan. They made a plan to cross into the land of Canaan and defeat the Israelites.

Meanwhile, Gideon had boldly taken charge. He arranged for messengers to go out to all the tribes asking for volunteers to come and join his army.

Gideon firmly believed that God was leading him, yet, as he reflected on the task that lay ahead, he was filled with anxiety.

"You say you want me to rescue Israel," he argued with God. "But can I be sure I have heard you right? Look, I am putting some wool down on the ground at the place where we thresh the wheat. If in the morning there is dew on the fleece but not on the ground, then I will know that you are indeed telling me to rescue my people."

In the morning, Gideon found the dew on the wool, just as he had asked. He picked it up and squeezed it; the water trickled through his hands, enough to fill a bowl.

Gideon looked, and he paused. "Don't be angry," he said to God, "but please may I ask for one more sign. This time, when I leave the wool out overnight, may I find the wool dry and the ground wet with dew."

It was done. With new courage, Gideon led his men to a place where they could see the Midianite camp. Men were swarming like locusts on the plain and there were camels too numerous to count. As he looked, he heard God saying that he himself did not need so large an army—he must announce that any who wanted could return home. Twenty-two thousand men left, and ten thousand stayed.

"You still have too many soldiers," said God. "So this time, take them to the stream to drink. Those who lie down to lap the water must be sent home. Those who scoop water up in their hands can stay."

Gideon was left with just three hundred men—three hundred who had shown in the test that they were always on the alert and ready for action. Secretly, he and his servant went down to the enemy camp. They overheard a conversation. "I had the funniest dream," a man was saying. "I dreamed a loaf of barley bread rolled into our camp and knocked a tent flat. What do you make of that?"

For Gideon, it was a sure sign: God was going to grant him victory.

That night, he divided his men into three groups, and each man had a trumpet and a jar that concealed the light of a torch burning within. He ordered the soldiers to creep to the edge of the camp and wait for his sign before they went into action.

It was a little before midnight. The enemy had just changed the guard, and the soldiers now on duty were nervously surveying the scene. Gideon's men swung into action. They blew a wild and terrifying blast on their trumpets, then smashed their jars and waved the torches high above their heads.

The enemy panicked. Some fought one another. The rest ran away. Gideon drove the Midianites out of the land, and his people lived in peace for forty years until he died.

Samson the Strong

Years passed after the mighty victories of Gideon. Once again, the Israelites began to worship other gods. Because of their disobedience, God allowed the Philistines to defeat them.

At that time, there lived a man named Manoah. His wife had been unable to bear any children. One day, an angel appeared to her and told her that she would be the mother of a son. He was to be dedicated to God, and his hair was to be left uncut through all his days as a sign of his special calling.

In due course, the woman bore Manoah a son, whom they named Samson.

His parents adored him and gave him everything he wanted. When he was a young man, he fell in love with a Philistine girl.

"I want to marry her," Samson declared. His mother and father eyed him warily. Why couldn't he have chosen a nice Israelite girl? Were they to blame for his ill-tempered demands? Had they given him too much? Had they failed to teach him to respect his people's God?

So the wedding was performed. Amid the celebration, the swaggering Samson set his guests a riddle to solve, with a prize for any who could find the answer.

"Boastful young foreigner doesn't deserve one of our girls," muttered some, and others who were listening agreed.

"Though I'm sure we can persuade her to find the answer for us," said one.

Within a week, the girl had wheedled the answer out of Samson. When the young men came and told it to him, he knew he had been betrayed. Samson saw his marriage was at an end and set about wreaking vengeance with great violence. He set fire to the Philistine cornfields and killed a thousand Philistine men with the jawbone of a donkey. Once, they thought they had him trapped inside one of their cities, but he ripped the city gate apart and strode away to freedom.

It was only when Samson fell in love with a beautiful Philistine girl named Delilah that his enemies saw a new chance.

"Find out what makes your handsome lover so strong," they pleaded, "and we will give you silver in abundance."

She asked, but Samson teased her with answers that were not true.

"How can you say you love me," she pouted, "and then mock me like this?"

So he explained: "My hair has never been cut—it is a sign that I have been dedicated to God. If I were to have my hair cut, and so break the vow, I would be as weak as anyone else."

Delilah smiled. "You are silly, not wanting to tell me that. Did you think I'd laugh at you and not want to see you anymore? You just come and lie down here."

While Samson lay sleeping, Delilah called her own people. They came and slashed away Samson's long, dark locks. He awoke in a rage, struggling for all his worth, but the Philistines captured him easily. They blinded him, then bound him in heavy bronze chains and set him to work like an ox, turning the great millstones in their prison.

Samson's Final Victory

The Philistines were delighted at having captured their great enemy Samson. Time passed, but the memory of their triumph remained fresh in their minds. "Let us hold a great ceremony in homage to our god Dagon," they agreed, "and let us give thanks for our victory."

Accordingly, a great crowd gathered in their temple. They offered sacrifices to their god and began a great feast of celebration.

"Our god has given us victory! Praise to god! Praise to god! Over our wicked enemy—praise to god!"

The people cackled and cheered and went on singing. The mood grew ever more festive, and then someone called out, "Bring that fool Samson in here, and let's have some fun with him."

A young boy led the haggard prisoner into the heart of the temple. The once-proud warrior stooped as he shuffled along, reaching out with his arms to fend off kicks and punches from the crowd.

"I love your hair," someone shrieked in Samson's ear. His tormentor grabbed a handful of locks and tugged at them sharply.

Samson staggered and felt his hair swing scratchily around his shoulders . . . his once-lovely hair, so roughly chopped and now growing into a shaggy mane. What a mess I've made of my vow to God, he thought.

The noise washed over him: Samson was deep in thought, his head bowed.

"Are you all right?" whispered the boy at his side.

"Help me put my hands on the pillars that hold up the building," Samson replied. "I need something to lean on."

He put one hand on each of the two great pillars of the building, then he prayed, "Sovereign Lord, please remember me. Please God, give me my strength just once more."

Samson pushed, slowly, relentlessly.

The pillars cracked under the force. "Let me die with the Philistines!" Samson shouted. Then the whole building collapsed on everyone.

With his death, Samson destroyed more of his people's enemies than he had done in all his lifetime.

The Story of Ruth

Time and again, the Israelites turned away from God and met with disaster.
Yet in the same period of Israel's history comes the gentle tale of a foreign
woman who agreed to worship the God of Israel and was blessed.

Long ago, there was a great famine. A man named Elimelech travelled with his wife and sons from the city of Bethlehem to the country of Moab. While they were there, the man died. His two sons grew up, and each married a girl from Moab. Some years later, the sons died, and Elimelech's widow, Naomi, was left to live with her daughters-in-law.

Time passed, and Naomi heard that there were once again good harvests in her homeland. She decided to return. "You girls, return to your homes," she said to her daughters-in-law. "May the Lord help each of you find a new husband from among your own people."

But one of the girls, Ruth, refused to leave. "I will go with you wherever you go," she wept. "Your people will be my people and your God will be my God."

When the two women reached Bethlehem, it was the time when the barley was being harvested.

"Let me go to the fields," said Ruth to Naomi. "I will gather the grain that the harvesters leave behind."

While she worked, the owner of the fields came by. His name was Boaz, and he was a relative of Naomi.

"Who is that young woman?" he asked one of his men.

"She is the foreign girl who has returned from Moab with Naomi," came the reply.

Boaz went up to Ruth and promised that she would be safe working in his fields. Ruth gathered a large quantity of grain for herself and for Naomi.

When the time for threshing the grain came, Naomi was worried, thinking about the lean winter months ahead. "It is only right that you should find a husband for yourself here," she said to Ruth. "Go to Boaz; remind him that he is responsible for taking care of his relatives."

Ruth did as she was told, and Boaz listened to her plea with kindness and secret delight, for Ruth was a lovely young woman. He made arrangements to take care of Naomi and married Ruth himself. In time, she bore him a son.

"You are so lucky!" said the local women to Naomi. "Your daughter-in-law has borne you a grandson, who will bring you joy now and take care of you when you are old."

The boy's name was Obed. He became the father of Jesse, who was the father of David, the great king of Israel.

The Story of Samuel

*As the years passed, the Israelites grew weary of the cycle of prosperity
and disaster that matched their times of obedience and disobedience to God.
Eventually, they cried out to be given a king who would rule them. The accounts
of that time begin with the story of the nation's last judge, Samuel.*

In the place called Shiloh was a little temple. Every year, those who were
faithful to God travelled there to offer sacrifices.

One year, a woman named Hannah journeyed there with her husband
Elkanah. She was childless. After they had made their sacrifices, Hannah
remained, weeping, as she prayed to God, silently telling of her longing to have
a son.

That year, Hannah became pregnant. She named her little son Samuel, and
she took great joy in caring for him until he was a toddler. Then, as she had
promised in her prayers, she took Samuel to Eli, the priest, in the temple.

Samuel stayed in Eli's care, and each year his mother returned, delightedly
bringing a little robe for him to wear.

Eli was pleased with Samuel, for he did his work in the temple carefully—
unlike Eli's two sons, who lived riotously and disgracefully. One night, Samuel
was sleeping in the special place where the Ark of the Covenant was kept.
Suddenly, Samuel heard a call.

Quickly, he jumped up and ran to Eli. "Here I am," he said.

"I didn't call you," replied Eli. "Go back to bed."

Samuel did so. Then he heard the voice again, and for a second time he ran
to Eli.

Again Eli sent him back to bed again, and Samuel lay down, puzzled.

The voice came a third time. "You did call me," Samuel said to Eli. "And here
I am."

Then Eli knew that it was God who was calling Samuel. "If you hear the
voice again," he instructed, "say this: 'Speak, Lord, your servant is listening.'"

So it was that by the flickering light of a flame, God told Samuel that Eli's
sons would not be allowed to take the elderly priest's place in the temple. Eli
heard the news and was sad. Yet in his heart, he knew that God had chosen
Samuel as the prophet for the people.

The Story of the Great Kings

Samuel led the people wisely. He travelled around the country, encouraging people to stay faithful to God and helping to settle disputes with his good judgments. But Samuel's sons did not follow his good example and, as he grew older, the people asked Samuel to appoint a king for them. In vain he argued that God was their king. What was Samuel to do?

In the region of Zuph, crowds were gathering on a hilltop to offer sacrifices to their God. They and all the townspeople were waiting expectantly for the great prophet Samuel to arrive to lead the ceremony.

Samuel was on his way, deep in thought. The day before, God had spoken to him: "Tomorrow I will send you a man from the tribe of Benjamin; anoint him as ruler of my people Israel. He will rescue them from their enemies." Then he heard footsteps—two men were approaching him. One was clearly a servant; the other, taller and remarkably handsome, had the appearance of a rich man's son.

"I am looking for the prophet," said the taller of the two. "Can you tell me where he lives?"

"I am he," replied Samuel, and all at once he felt that God's message had come true. "Go ahead to the place of worship on the hill. Then stay and eat with me this evening."

"We haven't come here for that," said the men. "In fact we wanted to ask you . . ."

"Tomorrow I will answer your questions," said Samuel. Then he smiled at them, for he knew with absolute certainty what he needed to say. "I know you are looking for donkeys that have been lost. Don't worry. They have already been found."

The young man and his servant exchanged glances. How did the prophet know their business?

"And you," Samuel went on, addressing the rich young man, "you are the one that the people of Israel are seeking."

"What do you mean?" The handsome youth was suddenly embarrassed and nervous. "I come from the smallest tribe of all. There is no reason why anyone should know who I am. . . ." His voice trailed off. Samuel had simply walked on ahead.

Nevertheless, the two did as they were told. The next day, Samuel took a jar of olive oil and performed a simple ceremony. He poured the oil onto the head of the tall young man. "Saul," he said to him, "the Lord has chosen you to be the ruler of his people." On that day, Saul knew that God was leading him.

Days passed. The young men returned home to a household where everything in their quiet world seemed to be as normal. Just as their adventure was fading to memory, an announcement came that all the people of Israel should gather, for Samuel wished to speak to them. He asked each tribe to step forward, for he was going to select a king for them. The people paraded past. But where was the young man? Where was Saul?

They found him hiding among the supplies. He was dragged out and led before the people. "Here is the man the Lord has chosen!" cried Samuel.

And the people shouted, "Long live the king!"

Saul the Warrior

"Long live the king!"

The sound of the people's cheering still rang in Saul's ears. A month had passed since the people of Israel had welcomed him as their leader, but here he was, back on his father's land, working in the fields. When he returned to the house, he heard weeping. "Messengers have come from the north saying the Ammonites have attacked them. They are begging for help."

So Saul called for volunteers to come from every tribe, and together they marched against the enemy and won a great victory.

Amid the rejoicing, Saul grew in confidence as the ruler of his people. Boldly he selected men to fight in his army. With advice from Samuel, he led them into battle against the Philistines from the west, and one victory followed another.

After some years, Samuel told Saul to battle against ancient enemies: the Amalekites from the southern wilderness, who had harassed the Israelites centuries before as they travelled out of Egypt. "Destroy that people," he said, "and all their wealth."

Saul won the battle but he did not destroy the spoils, and Samuel was furious. "You have not done as God wanted," he raged, "and so God has rejected you. The kingdom will be handed to another."

The two men parted, angry and sorrowful, and God spoke again to Samuel. "Choose for me another king, from among the sons of Jesse who lives in Bethlehem."

Samuel travelled to the little town among the hills, where sheep grazed on the thin grasses among the brambles and shepherd boys sat watching them.

Jesse welcomed the prophet warmly and introduced him to his son Eliab, who was tall and handsome.

Ah, here is a fine king, Samuel smiled to himself. But then, in his thoughts, he heard the clear voice of God: "I do not judge as people judge. They look at the outward appearance, but I look at the heart."

Samuel hesitated. "I'd like to meet all your sons," he said to Jesse. Even after he had spoken to six more, he was sure none of them was right. "Are these all your sons?" he asked.

"All except the youngest," said Jesse cheerfully. "He's out looking after the sheep."

The youngest was sent for: David, who came running back to the house, his eyes laughing, his homemade harp swinging from his shoulder.

Samuel knew at once that David was the one. He took a jar of oil and poured it over the head of the young man, declaring that David would be God's chosen king. With the future of the nation secure, Samuel lived out his days on the fringes of Saul's kingdom.

David and Goliath

King Saul was worried, very worried. His army was camped all around him on a hillside. A little brook trickled through the valley below. On the hill beyond, the enemy Philistine army was cheering—the army he could not defeat.

His soldiers gathered to watch as two soldiers walked out of the Philistine camp. One was a giant of a man, clad in gleaming bronze and wielding a massive spear. The other went in front of him carrying his shield.

"Slaves of Saul," shouted the giant, Goliath, "I dare you to pick someone to fight me. Beat me, and the whole army will surrender to you!" And then he laughed and laughed.

No one answered the challenge even though, day after day, Goliath stepped forward to taunt and mock them.

Then, one bright morning, someone walked into the Israelite camp, whistling a merry song. It was David, bringing food from home to his brothers at war.

David heard the challenge and grinned. "I'll go for it," he said. "With God on my side, how can I lose?"

Word of his boast reached Saul. When the king saw the young lad, he was dismayed. "You're just a boy, and Goliath has been a soldier for years."

"I've had years guarding the sheep in the hills," David replied. "I can fight lions and bears. . . . If God can save me from them, God can save me from Goliath."

Saul offered David his helmet and battle gear, but the boy found them too heavy. Instead, David set off down the hill with his slingshot and his stick. As he crossed the brook, he knelt down to pick up five smooth stones, which he put in his bag.

Goliath jeered when he saw him. "What's your stick for, boy?" he called. "Do you think I'm a dog?"

David smiled. "You've got a sword, a spear, and a javelin," he said, "but I come to fight you in the name of the God of Israel. And God's going to help me beat you."

Goliath strode forward. David ran toward him, grabbed a stone from his bag, fitted it into his sling, and hurled it at Goliath.

It hit the giant on the forehead, and he fell to the ground. In seconds, the victory was complete.

The Philistines fled, and David became the hero of the nation.

David the Outlaw

David became part of Saul's household. Every day, he played the harp, and the melodies brought joy and delight to his listeners.

David became so popular that Saul grew madly jealous. In a fit of rage he hurled a spear at the talented musician. He gave the young soldier dangerous assignments, hoping that the Philistines would kill him in battle.

But it was no good. David succeeded in all he did. Saul's daughter, Michal, fell in love with him and was delighted to be made his bride. Saul's eldest son, Jonathan, became a loyal friend and warned David of his father's schemes to kill him.

Soon David was forced to live as an outlaw—a bandit with his own following of soldiers, moving stealthily around the country to avoid being found and killed by his own king, his own people.

In the evenings, under the stars, he still made up his own songs. God saved him from wild animals. God had saved him from Goliath. And although, from time to time, he was driven to despair, in his heart he believed God would keep him safe always.

The Lord is my shepherd, I shall not want.
He makes me lie down in green pastures;
    he leads me beside still waters;
    he restores my soul.
He leads me in right paths
    for his name's sake.
Even though I walk through the darkest valley,
    I fear no evil;
for you are with me;
    your rod and staff—
    they comfort me.
You prepare a table before me
    in the presence of my enemies;
you anoint my head with oil;
    my cup overflows.
Surely goodness and mercy shall follow me
    all the days of my life,
and I shall dwell in the house of the Lord
    my whole life long.

Psalm 23

David the King

The victory years Saul had enjoyed were gone. His kingdom crumbled as foreign enemies closed in around him, and worry tormented him from within. "To whom can I turn now there is no prophet?" he lamented. "If only I could speak again with Samuel."

One of his advisers spoke to him quietly. "There is a woman in Endor who claims to be able to speak with the dead," the man whispered. "I know our laws forbid such practices, but in moments of desperation, perhaps . . ."

"Find her for me," ordered Saul grimly.

Among the weird shadows that flickered in the midnight hour, Saul watched as the woman conjured for him the spirit of Samuel. "Help me," pleaded Saul. "God no longer listens to me."

The pale figure of the prophet shook its head. "You have disobeyed the Lord in the way you have waged war," he warned. "After tomorrow's battle, you will join me beyond death's horizon."

The dreadful prophecy came true. When the news reached David— that Saul and Jonathan had been killed in a battle against the Philistines—he wept in grief.

Then God told him that the time had come for him to make himself king. The people from the tribe of Judah were quick to welcome him as their leader, but others wanted a king from Saul's family. There followed seven years of intrigue, murder, and treachery.

David was clever and cunning, and, through the struggle, God was with him. The day came when the people of Israel came to David and recognized that God had chosen him to be king.

Now he was leader, David decided to choose for himself a city to live in. He chose a fortress set on a hilltop and decided to capture it from its inhabitants, the Jebusites. The walls were strong and the hillsides up to them steep, but David had learned much stealth during his years as a bandit.

"In the fort," he said, "there is a tunnel that goes deep into the hill, and that leads to a spring of water. Who is brave enough to break into that tunnel out here on the hillside, and so climb up into the city itself?"

A small band of volunteers came forward, eager to prove themselves.

Their attack was swift and brutal, and the bodies of the Jebusites were strewn around the city.

The victory complete, David toured the settlement and made his plans. Here he would build his city, Jerusalem: a city of hewn stone and gleaming timber, with strong and beautiful buildings for himself, the king, and for his God. His kingdom was entering a golden age.

David and Bathsheba

One spring—the time of year when kings often went to war—David stayed in his city while his army went to fight. Alone, and with little to do, he had the leisure to sleep in the heat of the afternoon and stroll around the flat roof of the palace in the cool of the evening. One day after his nap, he saw a woman in a house not far away. She was having a bath, and he could see her lovely body.

David was fond of women. Since he had become king, he had taken several wives.

Who is that woman? he wondered, and he sent one of his servants to find out.

Her name was Bathsheba, and she was married. Her husband, Uriah, was one of the finest soldiers in David's army.

But I am king, thought David. So everything in the kingdom is mine if I want it. He sent orders that Bathsheba be brought to him, and he made love to her.

A little while later, news reached him that Bathsheba was pregnant—and it would soon become clear that Uriah could not be the father, for he was away fighting.

How inconvenient, thought David. Despite his arrogance, he was uneasy. How could he hide what he had done? At once, he commanded Uriah to return home from the wars. Uriah did so promptly, but declared that he would stay at the palace gate with the guards rather than go home to his wife, for that was the

right thing for a soldier to do. David tried to make him drunk, but Uriah still did not go home.

So David wrote a letter to the man in charge of the fighting. "Put Uriah in the front line," he ordered, "and abandon him there."

When the news of Uriah's death was brought to Jerusalem, Bathsheba mourned. David grimly waited until the time of mourning was over, and then sent for her to come to the palace and be his wife.

God was not pleased with what David had done. He sent his prophet Nathan to the palace.

"Listen to this tale," Nathan said to the king. "There was once a rich man who owned many cattle and sheep. Nearby lived a poor man, who had one lamb. He and his children loved it and treated it as their pet. One day, a visitor arrived at the rich man's home. The rich man didn't want to kill one of his own flock to feed the guest, so he took the poor man's lamb and served it as a meal."

"Outrageous!" exclaimed David. "That rich man ought to die."

"You are that man," said Nathan, "for you had Uriah killed and took his wife. You will be punished for this—the child Bathsheba is expecting will die."

David wept in sorrow, and his wailing song of grief echoed through his palace.

> Be merciful to me, O God,
>   because of your constant love.
> Because of your great mercy
>   wipe away my sins! . . .
> Create a pure heart in me, O God,
>   and put a new and loyal spirit in me.

Psalm 51:1, 10

Solomon the Wise

When Bathsheba became David's wife, she bore him a second son, and he was named Solomon. He grew up learning the law that God had given Moses, and David told him always to obey God's commands.

When David died, Solomon was still a young man. The thought of being king overwhelmed him, so he prayed to God, "Give me the wisdom I need to rule your people with justice, and to know the difference between good and evil."

God was pleased that Solomon had asked for this and promised to answer his prayer.

One day, two women came to King Solomon to ask him to judge between them. "Your Majesty," said one, "we two women live in the same house. Recently, I gave birth to a baby boy, and two days later this woman also had a son. Then, one night her baby died . . . and now she has stolen mine."

"No!" interrupted the other. "The living child is mine, and the dead one is yours."

Bitterly they began to argue in front of the king.

After a while, Solomon spoke. "Each of you claims the living child," he said. "So I need a sword to decide the matter."

When a soldier returned, Solomon ordered, "Cut the child in two and give each woman half of it."

The man lifted the gleaming blade.

"No!" screamed the first woman, "Give him to her, let her have him! He mustn't die!"

"Go ahead," said the other grimly. "Cut him in two."

The soldier looked at Solomon, awaiting his final order.

"Give the child to the first woman," said Solomon. "She is the real mother."

When the people heard of Solomon's decision, they were full of admiration and respect. "How wise is our king," they said to one another. "I would trust him to judge a dispute for me."

So began a long and prosperous reign for the king.

Solomon's Temple

One evening, as the setting sun cast its glow over the hills of Jerusalem, Solomon sat and wrote a letter to an old friend of his father, King Hiram of Tyre, a city on the coast to the north of Israel.

"You will remember that my father, David, always wanted to build a temple here in the city of Jerusalem," he wrote, "but was unable to do so as he had so many wars to fight. Now the Lord my God has given me peace on all the borders

of my country. I therefore wish to fulfil a promise I made to my father to build that temple."

Solomon paused. He walked to the window of the room and looked out. The city that his father had built with stone and timber supplied by the same King Hiram told a story of prosperity. Beyond, a broad hilltop stretched further to the north. That was the place his father had chosen for a temple that would shine with golden magnificence above the land all around, a building worthy of a great and mighty God. And it was for him, Solomon, to ensure that everything was done right. He returned to his writing.

"Please could you send some of your skilled woodcutters to Lebanon to cut down cedars for me. They will work alongside our people, and I will pay whatever you wish."

Hiram was delighted. "I am ready to do as you ask," he replied. "My men will bring the logs from Lebanon to the sea and float them in great rafts to a port of your choosing, so you will have less distance to take them over land to Jerusalem. You can have both cedar and pine and, in return, I simply ask that you provide food for the workers."

So it was that in the fourth year of Solomon's reign, four hundred and eighty years after the people of Israel left Egypt, work began on the Temple. It was immense and ornate, solid and strong, yet with the finest carving and a rich gold interior. In the innermost part of the Temple was a tiny room built to house the precious Ark of the Covenant.

When the Temple and all its furnishings were complete, the Ark was brought to Jerusalem in a ceremony that was both solemn and joyful. And Solomon said this prayer: "Praise the Lord who has given his people peace, as he promised he would. He has kept all the generous promises he made through his servant Moses. May the Lord our God be with us, as he was with our ancestors; may he never leave us, or abandon us; may he make us obedient to him, so that we will always live as he wants us to live, and keep all the laws and commands he gave our ancestors. . . . And so all the nations of the world will know that the Lord alone is God—there is no other."

The Story of the Northern Kingdom

The reign of King Solomon was glorious. After his death, however, the people of Israel argued among themselves. They rejected his son as king and set up their own ruler, a man named Jeroboam. So began the story of the northern kingdom of Israel. One of the early kings was the notorious Ahab.

❦

King Ahab of Israel listened lazily as a court scribe read aloud the chronicle listing of the rulers of the northern kingdom, and the story of how his people had broken with the traditions of Jerusalem, how they had built their own places of worship and how, as generations passed, they had been able to lay aside their old laws and bring in new customs. Easier customs, much more suitable for our times, thought Ahab. And my lovely queen Jezebel has been so dedicated in helping establish a proper respect for the mighty god Baal and the goddess Asherah. The followers of the God of Abraham have been reduced to a handful of eccentric prophets. How civilized!

To the king's irritation, one of the prophets arrived to speak with him that very day.

"I warn you," said the prophet Elijah, "in the name of the Lord, the living

God of Israel whom I serve, that there will be no dew or rain for the next two or three years . . . until I say so."

"Oh, nonsense," yawned Ahab. "Baal *is* the weather god, and the nations who worship him have brought in good harvests year after year. So go away, old man, or expect something very nasty to happen to you."

"Hide yourself," God warned Elijah. "Go beyond the Jordan. There, by the Cherith Brook, you will have water through the drought. Ravens will bring you food."

Elijah lived for many months this way. Then, as the famine grew more severe, he moved on to the town of Zarepheth. There he lived for two years, bringing great blessing to the household where he sheltered.

Meanwhile, back in his palace, King Ahab was listening as once again the chronicle that told the history of his reign was read aloud.

"Exactly how long has this drought been blighting us?" he asked.

"Three years," came the reply.

Ahab shook his head. "I still cannot believe that idiot Elijah believes in his God of Israel," he muttered. "But his wretched prophecy came true. How I hate him. . . ."

Elijah and the Fire from Heaven

King Ahab swore aloud as he stumbled along the dry riverbed. His fine leather sandals were not thick enough to protect him from the sharp stones, and he was angry.

"Curse that whining, half-wit Elijah, prophet of doom. It's three years since he showed up at my court saying that there would be no rain, and then he vanishes from the land, leaving me to go about like a farm hand trying to find pasture for the animals. I can only hope that Obadiah is having more success finding water than I am."

In the parched land, his servant Obadiah was jubilant. He hadn't found a blade of green grass, let alone a spring of water, but he had recognized someone he dearly wanted to see: Elijah, returning to see the king.

"Aha! The troublemaker has returned," called Ahab, when he caught sight of the prophet.

"I am no troublemaker," retorted Elijah. "You have made the trouble, by disobeying God and worshipping Baal. Now order the people of Israel to meet with me on Mount Carmel. Bring with you the prophets of Baal and of Asherah."

On the appointed day, Elijah addressed the people, asking, "How much longer will it take for you to make up your minds? If the Lord is God, worship him; but if Baal is God, worship him."

The people were silent. Elijah continued, "Here I am, the only prophet of the Lord. There are four hundred and fifty prophets of Baal. Bring two bulls to sacrifice. Let the Baal prophets take one, prepare it, and put it on wood, but not light a fire. I will do the same with the other. Then we will each pray to our god. The one that sends fire on the sacrifice is the one true God."

The prophets of Baal began their ceremony. They prayed until noon, when the sun shone fiercely in the clear azure sky. They danced and they raved and they worked themselves into a frenzy till the middle of the afternoon . . . but there was no fire.

Then Elijah summoned the people to come closer. He set about mending the altar to the Lord and laid the sacrifice on it. He had a trench dug all around the altar and had water poured over the sacrifice and the wood— enough to fill the trench.

Next, Elijah prayed to God. The Lord sent down fire so fierce it burned the sacrifice, the wood, the stones of the altar, and the earth around. The water boiled away in the sudden heat.

The people cried aloud, "The Lord is God; the Lord alone is God!"

The prophets of Baal were taken away and put to death. Meanwhile, out at sea, a wisp of a cloud uncurled itself in the sky and floated eastward toward the land. Then other clouds blew in, and the sky darkened as a chill breeze blew. Ahab jumped into his chariot and drove it furiously, hoping to reach home before the rainstorm; Elijah vanished into the wilderness, for Jezebel would soon be demanding his death.

Ahab and the Vineyard

King Ahab sat on the rooftop of his palace and watched his servants lay out the food for the evening meal. He gazed at various dishes that had been prepared—roast meat, freshly baked bread, and a pot of something that, he supposed, was meant to be vegetable stew.

"This isn't food for a king," he complained. "What is this sodden mess, and why can't you bring me something better?"

"O King," bowed a servant, "the land where the vegetables for the royal palace are grown has all but turned to dust, and as result . . ."

"Oh, don't bother me with excuses," moaned Ahab, and he turned away.

Not far from the palace, he could see a man still at work in a vineyard. His family was with him, gathering grapes by the basketful and laughing with delight.

There's a nice piece of land, thought Ahab. It would make a wonderful vegetable garden for me.

He asked to know who owned the vineyard. A man named Naboth was duly summoned to meet the king.

"I would like to buy your vineyard," declared Ahab. "You can have a better one in its place, or a fair price, whichever you prefer."

"No," replied Naboth, just as firmly. "I inherited the land from my ancestors. God forbid that you should have it." He turned and left.

Ahab glowered and sulked. He went to his room to lie down and refused to come out at the next mealtime. Queen Jezebel came to find out what was the matter. "Naboth won't sell me his vineyard," he whimpered.

Queen Jezebel knew how to soothe her husband. "Aren't you the king?" she purred. "Come on, cheer up. I'll make sure that vineyard is yours."

So she wove a tissue of lies, had Naboth accused of crimes and put to death.

Then she went back to her husband. "Naboth is dead. The vineyard is yours," she announced. At once he went off to survey his new property.

God sent Elijah to the king. "You have done a very great wrong," he warned. "You and your family will be punished for all your wrongdoing and will die shamefully."

At this, Ahab became gloomier than ever. For once, he truly repented and dressed in sackcloth as a sign.

"I will not punish Ahab in his lifetime," said God to Elijah, "for he is truly sorry."

So his dismal reign drifted on, until the day he was killed in battle.

The Chariot of Fire

Elijah walked toward the River Jordan, the young prophet Elisha at his side. A sudden gust of wind blew fiercely and the two men clutched their cloaks tightly.

Elijah fingered the rough wool of the cloak and shivered. He remembered how he had huddled into that same cloak years before, in a small cave high on Mount Sinai, where he had fled to escape Jezebel's murderous rage.

"I have always been faithful to you," he had confided to God, "but the people of Israel have broken their covenant with you, and now they are trying to kill me."

"Take courage," God had replied. "Return to the wilderness near Damascus, north of Israel, and anoint Hazael as king of Syria, Jehu as the new king of Israel, and Elisha as your successor. They will take care of your enemies."

Elijah had begun the task. When he first found Elisha, he had laid his cloak on him as a sign that he was to shoulder the work Elijah had done.

Now they were walking together. On the banks of the Jordan, Elijah took off his cloak, rolled it up, and struck the water with it. The water divided and the men crossed.

"I know the time has come for you to leave us," said Elisha. "When you go, let me receive the share of your power that will make me your true successor."

"That is difficult to grant," replied Elijah. "But if you see me as I go, it is a sign that you will have the power."

As they talked, there came a rushing sound, like wind passing through a gully. The sound grew to a tumult, and then horses of fire came galloping between the two men, pulling a chariot of flame. The wind swirled around, and Elisha saw his master being taken up in the chariot to heaven.

Elisha cried aloud as he watched him go. Then he looked to the ground. There was Elijah's cloak. The young prophet stooped and picked it up, and felt the rough wool. He knew now that God had given him the same power that had been given to Elijah.

The Miracles of Elisha

"Everyone talks of Elisha and the wonders he can perform."

The young girl from Israel was finding plenty to chatter about as she combed her mistress's hair into its elaborate ringlets.

"One of the stories is about the spring at Jericho. People were falling ill because the water was poisoned. Along comes Elisha, and it runs pure.

"Then there's another one about a widow who was so poor she was planning to sell her sons into slavery. All she had left was a little jar of olive oil. Elisha told her to collect as many jars as she could from her friends. She kept pouring from the one little jar, and it filled all the others. She sold the oil for a great deal of money.

"There's even a story that he brought someone back to life again. Sounds almost creepy, but it's true."

The wealthy woman smiled at the endless stream of stories her slave girl could tell. The chatter could be irritating, but she was cheerful and dutiful.

"And you know your husband, Naaman, has got a really bad bout of his skin disease," continued the girl. "Well, I think he should go to Elisha. He can cure anything. I know you must think I'm making things up—or that I believe things that are ridiculous—but it's worth a try."

Naaman was a general in the Syrian army—the very army that had captured the girl and made her a slave. But the man was suffering so much, and was so fearful of dying, that he was persuaded to go to the enemy country of Israel and plead for help.

When at last Naaman reached Elisha, the prophet simply sent his servant out with a message. "My master says, 'Go and wash seven times in the River Jordan and you will be cured.' "

Naaman was unwell, but that only made his temper worse. "I've travelled all this way," he raged, "and humiliated myself by coming to a people with whom we are often at war, and I get a stupid message via a servant. We've got excellent rivers in Syria. I don't need to come and add to my problems by dipping myself in the brown ooze they call a river."

Naaman's servants tried to soothe him. "If the prophet had asked you to do something difficult, you would have done it," they cajoled. "Why not try the remedy?"

Sulkily, Naaman went down to the Jordan. He washed seven times. As he wiped his skin dry, he looked at his arms in amazement. The skin was clear and healthy, like that of a child.

"Now I know there is no god but the God of Israel," he declared.

Jehu's Wild Ride

In the days of Elisha, Joram, son of Ahab, ruled Israel; his mother, Queen Jezebel, still continued her murderous campaign against the followers of Israel's God.

Elisha knew he had to carry on Elijah's work and anoint a new king as God had commanded, someone who could overthrow the royal family and root out every wickedness. God's choice was a young soldier named Jehu.

"Here comes the boy racer," laughed Jehu's fellow officers, as they gathered together for a military meeting. Jehu was driving his chariot at full speed toward them, whooping gleefully. At the last moment, he flicked the reins to make the horses rear up, and the chariot swung around to a perfect stop just inches away from his admiring comrades.

As they talked about the kingdom and its wars, Elisha arrived. He took Jehu aside and anointed him with oil, following God's command, and he told Jehu he must kill Joram and all Ahab's family.

When Jehu's comrades heard what had happened, they cheered. "Jehu is king!" they called out triumphantly. And "You can count on our support," they whispered quietly. "We are all weary of Jezebel and her witchcraft."

One of the king's guard, on duty on his watchtower, was the first to spy the rebellion. "I see men riding up," he called out. A messenger was sent to find out who they were, but Jehu commanded the man to fall in behind him. A second messenger was sent, but he, too, fell in behind the charioteers.

"The man is not returning," warned the guard, "but the leader of the group is driving his chariot like a madman. Only Jehu drives that way. It must be him!"

King Joram went in his chariot to meet Jehu. "Do you come in peace?" he demanded.

"How can there be peace," Jehu answered, "when we still have all the witchcraft and idolatry that your mother, Jezebel, started?"

"Treason!" screamed Joram. He wheeled his chariot away, but Jehu slotted an arrow into his bow and pulled with all his might. The arrow struck Joram in the back and pierced his heart.

Jehu rode on to Jezreel, where Jezebel had heard of her son's assassination. She waited at the palace window, beautiful and terrifying in her regal finery. "Murderer! Why are you here?" she hissed at the young charioteer.

Jehu looked up and saw courtiers at the windows near the queen.

"Who is on my side?" shouted Jehu to them. "Throw her down!"

The cheers and jeers of the rebels drowned Jezebel's final, awful shriek as she fell. Jehu entered the palace to show that he was the next king. When servants went to collect the queen's body, it had been eaten by dogs, all except the skull and the bones of her hands and feet.

With ruthless determination, Jehu wiped out the remainder of Ahab's family, and with them the worship of Baal.

The Faithful Prophet

After Jehu's reign, the people of Israel once again neglected God's laws. Although outwardly they appeared to worship God, their lifestyle was full of greed and selfishness.

God chose a prophet named Hosea to warn them. He was a gentle and kindly man, but God told him to marry a woman who loved wild and extravagant living. She bore him children, but soon ran off with many other men, taking her children with her.

One day, their little girl was leaning on a cushion by the window, watching the street below. She was bored. Her mother had bought her all the toys she wanted, and servants prepared wonderful meals, but she was supposed to stay indoors most of the time so no one could snatch her away.

Then, among the crowds she saw the kind face of someone she knew. "Father, Father!" she called.

From the next room, her brothers came running. "Where is he? What's he doing?"

Hosea waved up at them. "I love you," he called. "Please tell your mother to come and see me," he asked, trying to blink back the tears in his eyes.

So she did, and the two grown-ups talked and cried together. Soon they once again lived as a family.

Months later, the little girl was sitting at the window of her parents' house, listening as hard as she could to what her father was saying to the crowd in the street below.

"People of Israel, change your ways. Look hard at the way you live . . . the way you spend your money, the way you treat those who work for you, the way you treat your family and the people in your community. Think again of the laws our people have been given to guide them. Turn back to God, who is as loving as . . . as a husband who forgives his wife."

The crowd knew Hosea's story. Some jeered. Others smirked. A few looked thoughtful. Perhaps what Hosea was saying was worth listening to.

"Will God really forgive wicked people, just like you forgave Mother?" the little girl asked her father that evening.

"I believe so," said Hosea. "And I believe that from the descendants of the good king David, God will one day choose a leader who will lead us in the way of righteousness."

Israel, I will make you my wife;
I will be true and faithful;
I will show you constant
   love and mercy
and make you mine forever.

Hosea 2:19

The Story of Jonah

The story of Jonah is set in Israel, in the time when Assyria was the nation's most feared enemy.

❧

Jonah was a man in a hurry. A prophet in a hurry. A man on the run. God's command to him echoed in his mind.

"Go to Nineveh."

It was the last thing Jonah wanted to do. The capital city of the Assyrians was a byword for wickedness; the Assyrians were his people's worst enemies. He kept on running.

"Go to Nineveh, and warn the people that I, God, have seen their evil doings."

Let God find another way to get his message to Nineveh, thought Jonah. He himself was on the way to Joppa, down on the coast.

When he arrived there, he boarded a ship that would take him as far away from Nineveh as it was possible to go. That night, he lay down in the hold of the ship, listening to the waves and the creaking timbers.

The sailors on deck watched the evening sky darken and night clouds fly past the moon. They shifted warily as the wind blew harder and the swell grew deeper.

Then waves crashed over the boat, and suddenly everyone was hard at work, desperate to keep the ship upright in the towering, menacing sea.

"Who can have angered the gods to bring such a storm upon us?" they demanded to know, and they cast lots to find out. The answer came: Jonah.

"I'm sorry; it is my fault," Jonah trembled. "I am from Israel, and I am running away from my God . . . you will have to throw me into the sea."

The captain took charge. "It will go badly for us if we kill this man. Keep him here and row for shore," he commanded.

It was no use. The sea hissed and shivered above the ship like a monster about to devour them.

"Very well then," said the captain sadly. "Throw the man overboard."

"May God forgive us!" they shouted, as they hurled their passenger into the sea.

The storm ceased immediately. Down went Jonah into the water. There, in the murkiest deep, a huge fish opened its mouth and swallowed him.

It was darker than the hold of the ship, dark and awful. Yet Jonah knew that God had saved him. There, in the belly of the fish, he promised once again to be faithful to God.

Jonah and the Castor Oil Plant

Three days and three nights passed, and then the fish spewed Jonah up onto a beach. At God's command, Jonah went to Nineveh and walked all through the city, calling to the people.

"Mend your ways before it is too late! In forty days, God will destroy your city, all because of your wickedness."

The people turned their heads. They looked; they listened. They spread the word of Jonah's warning.

The news reached the king. "This is dreadful news!" he exclaimed. "Yet how clearly I see that we must make changes immediately." He gave orders for the whole city to dress in sackcloth as a sign of their sorrow, and for everyone to mend their ways.

The city was spared, and Jonah was furious.

"I knew it! I knew it! God has forgiven my enemies! God has shown mercy to the enemies of my people." And he shouted to God, "Why are you always so loving and merciful and kind? Why can't you punish those who deserve to be punished? I'd rather die than see the Assyrians forgiven."

He went out to a hill above the city and built himself a little shelter. All at once, a plant grew up, and its leaves shaded Jonah from the hot sun. Jonah was delighted.

What a lovely plant, he thought, as its leaves wafted cool air over his face. I cannot remember having such a happy day basking in the sun.

But the next day, a worm attacked the plant, and it died. The sun rose and a hot wind blew. Jonah began to complain. "My poor plant," he wailed. "How I miss its lovely leaves and its cool shade." He looked up to God. "Without my plant," he moaned, "I'd rather die."

Then God spoke to him again. "The plant grew in one night and died the next. Yet you feel sorry for it. So why shouldn't I feel sorry for Nineveh and its thousands upon thousands of children and all its animals?"

The Story of the Southern Kingdom

*Years had passed since the time of Solomon. King Hezekiah now ruled
the little kingdom of Judah that had stayed faithful to the kings of Jerusalem.
He put great energy into ensuring that the worship of God in the Temple
was conducted in the right way. While he was busy, he was happy, but when
the busy time was over, he had time on his hands—time to worry.*

❦

K ing Hezekiah listened sullenly as a courtier listed the entertainments that
could be provided to cheer him that evening.

"I know that your advisers would like to spend a little time bringing you up
to date with the political situation," said the man.

"It's always bad news," snapped Hezekiah, "and it's the same news today as
yesterday. The kingdom of Israel has fallen to the invading Assyrians. It's only a
matter of time before they march into Judah. Do my advisers think I don't know
that?"

The courtier paused. "A Temple official has prepared the report on the
amount of gold and silver it holds in its treasury. With such wealth, you may be
able to bargain with the Assyrians for peace."

What a depressing thought, sulked Hezekiah.

The courtier took a deep breath. "One of the junior officers in the army has expressed a wish to speak to you about a very unusual idea. He believes it is possible to cut a new tunnel through solid rock so the people of Jerusalem will be able to get to a supply of fresh water, even if they are besieged. I know it sounds ridiculous, but . . ."

Hezekiah was delighted. He listened intently to the plan and soon set about the great task of fortifying the city and building the tunnel to protect his people from the Assyrians.

> "Be determined and confident, and don't be afraid of the Assyrian emperor or of the army he is leading. We have more power on our side than he has on his. He has human power, but we have the Lord our God to help us and to fight our battles."
>
> 2 Chronicles 32:7—8

The Siege of Jerusalem

Sennacherib, the emperor of Assyria, commanded a mighty army. Having swept through the kingdom of Israel, he led his fighting men to the kingdom of Judah. Relentlessly, they began destroying its cities. Desperate for peace, King Hezekiah sent all the silver and gold from the Temple and the palace treasury. But the Assyrians did not stop their attack. By the time they came to Jerusalem, they had celebrated several victories.

Now they were camped outside Jerusalem. On the walls, a mother and her children wept as they heard the enemy's messenger call out his threat.

"Give in," he shouted in the language of the listeners. "Your king can't save you, and neither can your God. Surrender to the emperor, and you will be resettled in a fertile land as good as the one you have now."

"Will the same thing happen to us here as happened at Lachish?" sobbed the boy. "They have the same battering rams to knock the walls down."

"Haven't they used up all their arrows?" wailed the little girl.

The mother wiped her tears away. "We managed to escape from the prison camp," she said. "If God took care of us then, God can take care of us now."

Their cousin in whose house they were staying in Jerusalem was even more hopeful. "King Hezekiah has made excellent preparations," she said, as she filled the children's drinking mugs generously full of water. "The springs of water outside the city have all been blocked, so Sennacherib's army has to carry water in. But there's a tunnel inside the city that leads to a pool where fresh water wells up, so we are in no danger of running out."

King Hezekiah was in the Temple, praying: "O Lord, the God of Israel, seated on your throne above the winged creatures, you alone are God, ruling all the kingdoms of the world. You created the earth and the sky. Now, Lord, look at what is happening to us . . . rescue us from the Assyrians, so that all the nations of the world will know that only you, O Lord, are God."

The prophet Isaiah was giving his servant a message from God to tell the king. "This is what the Lord has said about the Assyrian emperor: 'He will not enter this city or shoot a single arrow against it. No soldiers with shields will come near the city, and no siege mounds will be built around it. He will go back by the same road he came, without entering this city. I, the Lord, have spoken. I will defend this city and protect it, for the sake of my own name and because of the promise I made to my servant David.' "

That night, disaster came to the Assyrian camp. Death swept through it like an avenging angel, and thousands of soldiers breathed no more. Sennacherib had little choice. He withdrew all his troops and returned to his own city of Nineveh.

The Fall of Jerusalem

King Hezekiah died in peace. His son, and later his grandson, came to the throne. They neglected the worship of the Temple, and it was the next king, Josiah, who inspired his people to live again as God's people.

But after the time of Josiah, more wars threatened. On Judah's northern borders, Assyria was growing weaker, but to the northeast the rulers of Babylon were conquering an empire for themselves.

"We cannot hope to beat the Babylonians," warned the prophet Jeremiah. "At "At least let us talk with them and see if we can offer our surrender. That way, at least, we may be able to keep our lives. Perhaps our Temple will be spared."

No one wanted to listen. The rulers of Judah regarded him as a traitor, and they scorned him and continued to treat him cruelly. At the same time, they fought in vain against the mighty army of King Nebuchadnezzar of Babylon.

After the battle, Jeremiah met with his countrymen and soon learned what had happened.

"When King Zedekiah saw that he could no longer defend the city, he tried to escape with some of his household. Nebuchadnezzar's troops caught up with them."

"His family was killed, and he himself blinded and taken to Babylon."

"And the warnings you gave us, Jeremiah . . . how terrible and true they were."

Jeremiah lifted his eyes to Jerusalem's high hill. The beautiful and ancient Temple had been torn down. Its bronze and gold and silver had been carried away.

Jeremiah looked down to the valley below. Many of the people of Judah were being led away to away to live in exile in Babylon.

Jeremiah looked around. "We are only poor people," said those near him. "The Babylonians have no use for us. We can stay here, but we must make a living on the devastated land."

"This is all so sad," wept Jeremiah. "Yet God is God, and we are God's people."

The thought of my pain, my homelessness, is bitter poison;
    I think of it constantly and my spirit is depressed.
    Yet hope returns when I remember this one thing:

The Lord's unfailing love and mercy still continue,
    Fresh as the morning, as sure as the sunrise.
    The Lord is all I have, and so I put my hope in him.

Lamentations 3:19–24

The Story of the Jews in Exile

The people of Judah were filled with dismay when they were led away as exiles.
Would the God whom they had worshipped in the Temple in Jerusalem take
care of them in faraway Babylon, among people who worshipped other gods?

❦

King Nebuchadnezzar was the great king of Babylon, and his word was law. He ordered a huge golden statue to be made, and commanded the officials in his empire to come and stand before it. There, a herald made the announcement: "When the king's musicians play, all of you must bow down and worship the golden statue. Those who disobey will be thrown into a burning fiery furnace."

The music rang out. The people all bowed down: all, that is, except three.

Noticing this, some people from Chaldea went to the king. "Three Jews who serve in your government have ignored your command," they whispered. "O King, Shadrach, Meshach, and Abednego do not worship your golden statue."

King Nebuchadnezzar ordered the young men to be brought before him.

"Is this accusation true?" he thundered. "For if it is, you will be thrown into a burning fiery furnace, and what god will save you then?"

Shadrach, Meshach, and Abednego replied, "If the God we serve can save us, then the God we serve will save us. And even if our God does not, then know for sure that we will still not worship your statue."

King Nebuchadnezzar's fury rose. "Make the fire seven times hotter than usual," he ordered. "Throw these men into the flames!"

The guards who carried out the order were burned to death. The men from Chaldea were burned to death. But an angel from God came into the furnace and drove the flames outward, so that in the heart of the fire it was as if a cool wind were blowing. The three young men began to sing to the Lord their God.

King Nebuchadnezzar sprang to his feet. "What is this I see?" he cried. "Surely I had three men thrown into the furnace. Yet now I see four, and one looks like an angel." He stepped forward. "Shadrach, Meshach, and Abednego, come out!"

The king's officials gathered in amazement: the young men were not burned at all.

Then King Nebuchadnezzar made a proclamation: "Blessed be the God of Shadrach, Meshach, and Abednego. Let no one speak disrespectfully of their God, or I will punish them severely, for no other god can save like this."

"May you be blessed, Lord,
    God of our ancestors,
be praised and extolled forever. . . .

"For he has saved us from the
    burning fiery furnace,
rescued us from the heart
    of the flame.
Give thanks to the Lord,
    for he is good,
for his love is everlasting."

From Daniel 3:52, 88–90

Daniel in the Pit of Lions

The Babylonian king was happy to choose talented people from among the exiles to serve in his government. Among them was a gifted man from Judah—Daniel. He was so admired that, when the Medes and Persians captured Babylon in the time of Nebuchadnezzar's son, the new ruler, Darius, kept him as an adviser.

It was Daniel who occupied the thoughts of another adviser as he marched grimly home one evening. "The king is considering putting that Judean exile Daniel in charge of all one hundred and twenty of his governors," he fumed.

"The job you wanted," cooed his wife. "So . . . perhaps you'll need to talk with the other governors about how to handle the situation." She smiled a knowing smile.

The man began to scheme the very next day. He was the one who led the governors to a special audience with Darius. "King Darius, may Your Majesty live forever. We have agreed that Your Majesty should ensure that everyone in the empire is completely loyal to you. We have agreed that you should issue an order that for thirty days no one is to request anything from any god or human being other than yourself. Anyone who breaks the order should be thrown into a pit of lions."

Darius was flattered to think they had his interests at heart and he signed the order in the customary way—"a law of the Medes and Persians, which cannot be changed."

"And now," said the governor to his fellow conspirators, "we need only wait."

They were right. Soon they spied Daniel going to the window of his house that faced toward Jerusalem. There he knelt and prayed to God.

The governors rubbed their hands with glee.

Darius protested when he heard the news. "Daniel is my finest administrator. I know that he is completely loyal. He does not have to submit to this new law to prove that."

"But you signed the law yourself," argued the governors. "The terms are clear. It is a law of the Medes and Persians, which cannot be changed."

Darius saw he was trapped. He gave the order that Daniel be thrown into the pit of lions but, as Daniel was led away, he whispered, "May your God, whom you serve so loyally, rescue you."

In the morning, he raced to the pit. "Daniel," he called, "has your God saved you?"

"May Your Majesty live forever," came the reply. "God sent an angel to protect me, for God knows my loyalty to you is unfailing."

Darius was overjoyed. He gave orders for Daniel to be hauled from the pit.

Then he spoke to his soldiers. "Here are the names of the men who accused Daniel," he snapped. "Bring them, with their wives and children, and throw them into the pit."

While the lions greedily tore the bodies to pieces, Darius wrote a message to all his people: "I command that throughout my empire everyone should fear and respect Daniel's God. He is a living God, and he will rule forever."

The Story of the Returning Exiles

When the Persians took control of the Babylonian empire, life changed for the exiles in Babylon. Their new rulers were happy to let them return to their old homeland, if they so wished. Some made the long journey back home. But their beloved city in Jerusalem was now in ruins and lying neglected—no one had repaired the wall or gates since they had been destroyed. This news eventually spread to Jews elsewhere.

Pull yourself together, Nehemiah told himself crossly, as he wiped the tears from his eyes. You have work to do. Nehemiah was a Jew who served as a wine steward in the royal household of Persia in the city of Susa.

But he couldn't get Jerusalem out of his mind. He was still brooding four months later, when he took wine as usual to the room where the Emperor Artexerxes was dining with his wife.

The emperor sipped from his goblet thoughtfully, without seeming to notice his servant's presence. Then he looked up. "You must have had some bad news recently, Nehemiah," he said. "I have never seen you look so sad."

"Your Majesty," Nehemiah replied, "how can I help looking sad when the city of my ancestors, the once-beautiful Jerusalem, is still in ruins?"

"I see," said the emperor. "Is there any way I can help?"

Nehemiah let his thoughts fly to God in a prayer, and then he replied, "Your Majesty, please allow me to return to my homeland of Judah and help rebuild the city."

The emperor granted his request. He also arranged for him to travel with an escort through the lands that lay between the splendid city of Susa and the ruins that were Jerusalem, and for him to be supplied with timber to help in the rebuilding plan.

Nehemiah returned and rode around the city by night, inspecting the ruins and deciding what needed to be done. Then he set about persuading the inhabitants of Jerusalem to start the work of rebuilding their city.

The people of Jerusalem were soon enthusiastic, and they set to work on the walls of the city. However, other people who lived nearby were angry and scornful. Among those who opposed the work were the people known as Samaritans who had never gone into exile. They began to plan an attack on Jerusalem.

Nehemiah heard of the plot but was not discouraged. God heard my prayer when I was waiting at table, he thought cheerfully. God is much greater than any of our enemies.

He arranged for the workers to be divided into two teams. At any one time, some were building, while others stood guard, dressed for battle and carrying spears, shields, and bows. Every member of the building team carried a sword. A man with a bugle was appointed to stay close to Nehemiah, ready to sound the alarm if needed.

In this way, Nehemiah helped restore his country, and with it, the worship of God and an honest and peaceful way of life for his people.

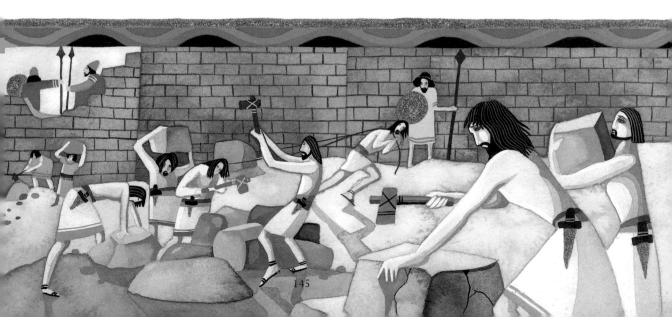

The Story of Esther

*This story, set in the heart of the Persian empire, tells of how the people
from Judah—known as the Jews—survived a plot to massacre them.*

Queen Esther tugged at the royal robes she had chosen to wear. They felt
loose and baggy. Perhaps the three days without eating hadn't been such a
good idea. Then she looked in the mirror and her heart sank still further. Her
face had definitely become thinner, and it made her look much older.

"Today, of all days, when I have to please the king the moment he sets eyes on
me . . ." she agonized. "And he chose me as his queen because of my beautiful
looks."

Her servant girl came up and clasped her hand. "We have all prayed so much
these last three days," she said. "You look very, very lovely . . . but most of all, we
trust that God will look after you now."

Esther felt her knees trembling as she left her own rooms in the palace. She
might never walk that way again. To approach the king without being sent for was
punishable by death. But her uncle Mordecai and her people, the Jews throughout
the Persian empire, had no one else who had a hope of saving them from the
massacre that had been ordered by the king's governor, the cruel Haman.

Esther reached the inner courtyard. Fear could not help her now. She lifted
her head and looked bravely toward the king's throne. He was sitting facing her.

She met his eyes. What would he choose: to welcome her, or to order her
execution?

Slowly, definitely, he lifted his royal golden staff as a sign she was welcome.
Esther smiled gratefully. She walked forward to touch the tip of the staff. "If it
pleases Your Majesty," she said, "I would like you and Haman to be my guests
tonight at a banquet I am preparing for you."

"My dear and lovely queen," replied the king, "it will be a pleasure for us to
attend."

Esther lowered her dark eyes and blinked back tears of relief. The first stage
of her plan had succeeded.

Mordecai and Haman

Esther's evening reception was a great success. The king offered her anything she wanted, but she made no request, other than to ask for a second banquet with the king and Haman the next night. Haman left the palace in high spirits, confident that the king trusted and valued him more than anyone else. "My career is going excellently," he exclaimed to his family and friends. "Just one little nuisance to get rid of: that Jew Mordecai who hangs around the palace. I hate him and all his people."

"Oh, if he likes hanging around, why not have him hanged?" joked his wife. Everyone laughed, and Haman immediately ordered a gallows to be built.

The king enjoyed Esther's banquet, too, but that night he couldn't sleep. So he arranged for some records of the empire to be brought and read aloud to him. He heard again the story of a plot to assassinate him some time before, and how it had been foiled.

"Who was it who warned me of the plot," he asked drowsily, "and how was he rewarded?"

"It was the Jew, Mordecai," came the reply. "There is no record of any reward."

The king was dismayed. The next morning he asked Haman's advice. "There is someone whom I feel deserves public acclaim," he announced. "What should I do for him?"

Haman smiled a broad smile. His dream was coming true—the king wished to make him a hero and he was being allowed to choose his own reward.

"Oh, it is important to put on a bit of a show," he said. "You must show your people how you reward those you consider worthy. I think the man should be dressed in royal robes and led in a fine procession through the city."

"Excellent," said the king. "Go and arrange to do this for Mordecai."

"Mordecai?" asked Haman faintly. "Er . . ."

"Thank you," said the king.

Angry and humiliated, Haman did as he was ordered. In his heart, he delighted that his strategy to order the massacre of the Jews was already in hand, and the day for it approaching fast.

That evening, he returned for a banquet with the king and queen.

"Now, Queen Esther, tell me what it is you want," the king said again.

Esther replied, "I wish that I may live and that my people may live. As it is, there is a plan to destroy us all."

"Outrageous!" exclaimed the king. "And who is behind it?"

"It is Haman," replied Esther with icy calm.

The king ordered that Haman be hanged on the gallows he himself had built. On the day arranged for the massacre, the Jews were given leave to defend themselves. In this way, Queen Esther saved her people.

The New Testament

The second section of the Bible is known as the New Testament. It is a collection of over twenty books, all of which talk about the life and message of the man known as Jesus. He lived in the land of Palestine about two thousand years ago, and the books were written by his followers in the hundred or so years immediately after his death. The language used for writing at that time was Greek. Fragments of very early writings still exist, and there is an abundance of careful copies that are also very old.

The first four of the books of the New Testament are called the Gospels, and they are four accounts of the life of Jesus, as told by Matthew, Mark, Luke, and John. After the Gospels comes the book of Acts, which is an account of what happened to his followers next. Most of the other books are letters written by leading Christians to groups of new followers, helping them to understand more about Jesus.

The stories in this book are drawn mainly from the Gospels, with a glimpse into how the story of Jesus began to spread to all the world, with its appealing message of how everyone is welcome in God's kingdom.

The Story of the Birth of Jesus

Two books of the Bible tell of the time when Jesus was born. They are known as the Gospel of Matthew and the Gospel of Luke. Not much is known about how the Gospel of Matthew came to be written. However, ancient traditions say that Luke was careful to gather as much information as he could for his book from people who had witnessed the events. They say that Luke spoke with Jesus' mother, Mary, and that she told him of her memories.

Among the hills of Galilee lies a town called Nazareth—a plain little town of white-walled houses surrounded by fields that in springtime are filled with flowers.

Long ago, a girl called Mary lived there. She was old enough to be getting married, and her family had arranged for her to marry a man named Joseph.

"He is a good man who always tries to do what is right," they said, "and his family can trace their ancestors back to the nation's great King David."

Mary could look ahead to a pleasant and contented life.

Then, one day, an angel appeared to her.

"Peace be with you," said the angel. "The Lord is with you and has greatly blessed you."

Mary was alarmed. Who was this amazing visitor, and what message was hidden in those words?

"Don't be afraid, Mary," said the angel. "God has chosen you to be the mother of a child, whom you are to call Jesus. He will be a great man. People will call him the Son of the Most High God. God will make him a king like his ancestor David, and his kingdom will never end."

Mary was utterly perplexed. "How can this be?" she said. Then a sensible, practical question occurred to her. "I am not yet married; how can I become a mother?"

"God will make it happen," replied the angel. "There is nothing that God cannot do."

In her heart, Mary knew she wanted to live all her life in obedience to God. She felt at peace as she gave her answer. "Then let it be as you say," she replied.

Later, as she reflected on the role that had been given her, she was moved to utter a song of praise:

"My heart praises the Lord;
  my soul is glad because of God my Saviour,
  for he has remembered me, his lowly servant!
From now on all people will call me happy,
  because of the great things the Mighty God has done for me.
His name is holy."

Luke 1:46–49

Mary, Joseph, and the Dream

"Mary is expecting a baby."

The news that was brought to Joseph shattered his dreams, his everyday, honest dreams. The lovely girl he was to marry was pregnant . . . but the baby was not his.

He spent long hours worrying. Just what is the right thing to do now, he wondered. I don't want the girl I love to be disgraced, but how can I marry her when she is expecting someone else's baby?

At last he made a decision. "I will have to break off the engagement," he said. "But I will take great care to do so quietly. That way, there will be no scandal, and perhaps each of us can build a new future for ourselves."

Then, in the night, he had a dream—an angel of God appeared to him.

"Joseph, descendant of David," said the messenger, "don't be afraid to take Mary as your wife. The child she carries has been conceived by God's Holy Spirit. She will have a son, and you will name him Jesus. He will lead people back to the way of living as God wants, the way of doing what is good and right."

Joseph awoke with new hope and new resolve. He married Mary, as the angel had told him to, and took care of her through the months when her baby was growing within her.

The Stable in Bethlehem

The land where Mary and Joseph lived was part of the great Roman empire. At the time when Mary was expecting her baby, the emperor Augustus ordered that all people under his rule go and register their names with his officials. By this means he would discover the precise number of people from whom he could demand taxes—the money he needed for armies, conquests, and a rich, luxurious lifestyle.

The order said that everyone must go to the town from which their family came. So it was that Joseph went from Nazareth in Galilee to Bethlehem in Judea, for this was the birthplace of his ancestors and of King David himself.

Mary travelled with him. The journey was long and very tiring, for her baby was soon to be born. But reaching their destination brought no comfort, for in the little town, all the rooms for travellers were full.

Mary grew anxious. "I know that the baby will soon be born," she cried. "We must find somewhere for me to lie down."

In desperation, the two sought shelter in a stable. There, the baby was born—a son, just as the angel had said.

Mary wrapped her baby tenderly in a soft blanket held in place with swaddling clothes, and she cradled him in a manger.

The Shepherds and the Angels

On the hillsides around Bethlehem, some shepherds were spending the night in the fields watching over their flocks. They huddled together for warmth and companionship, and drew their cheerful, homespun cloaks around their shoulders.

Suddenly, the night was filled with beauty, with a radiance that was brighter than the stars and clearer than the moon. There, before them, stood an angel of God.

The shepherds cowered in fear, cringing among the rocks and briars. But then the angel spoke in a voice as gentle as it was joyful.

"Do not be afraid," said the angel. "I bring you good news—good news for all the world. This very day, in David's town of Bethlehem, your Saviour has been born. God's promised king has come—the Messiah, the Christ.

"I will tell you what to look for, so that you will know that what I say is true. You will find the baby wrapped in swaddling clothes and lying in a manger."

Then a great crowd of angels appeared, singing praises to God with a clear and lovely melody, a tune from heaven to bring joy to the earth.

"Glory to God in the highest heaven,
and on earth peace, goodwill among people."

Luke 2:14

Then the angels went, and the night was as before: dark, cool and with a soft breeze blowing.

The shepherds began to murmur among themselves. "Let us go and see," they agreed.

So they hurried off to Bethlehem. They found Mary and Joseph and saw the baby lying in the manger. They described what they had seen, and as they left, sang to God.

Mary was left to wonder at all that had happened.

159

Old Simeon

The time came for Joseph and Mary to take the baby Jesus to the Temple in Jerusalem, for it was a custom of the Jewish people to present every firstborn son to God in this way.

There was a man named Simeon living in the city. Simeon loved God with all his heart, and he believed that God would not let him die before he had seen the Messiah spoken of in the books of the prophets.

One day, he felt that the voice of God was telling him to go to the Temple. He was there when Mary and Joseph arrived with the child Jesus.

Simeon walked forward. "May I hold the child?" he asked.

As he took the child in his arms, he was filled with joy and spoke these words:

> "Now, Lord, you have kept your promise,
>   and you may let your servant go in peace.
> With my own eyes I have seen your salvation,
>   which you have prepared in the presence of all peoples:
> A light to reveal your will to the Gentiles
>   and bring glory to your people Israel."

Luke 2:29–32

"This child is chosen by God to do great things among our people," he said. "But there will be some who turn against him. When that happens, sorrow, like a sharp sword, will break your heart."

Then an old and wise woman named Anna saw the child, and she, too, spoke of the great things he would do.

Once again, Mary was left wondering.

Jealous King Herod

Jesus was born in the town of Bethlehem in Judaea during the time when Herod was king in Jerusalem.

Herod was a man greedy for power and haunted by the fear that it would be wrenched from him. He had spent years scheming to persuade his Roman overlords to let him rule the land of the Jews. In that time, he had ruthlessly arranged the murders of all who threatened his plans—his sons and his wife among them.

To the city of Jerusalem came travellers from the East, men who studied the stars. "Where is the baby born to be king of the Jews?" they asked. "We have seen his star rise on the eastern horizon and we have come to worship him."

Herod heard of their quest, and terror gripped him. He summoned his advisers. "I know that our prophets have spoken of a Messiah, of a king whom God will send our people. Do they also know where this Messiah will be born?"

"Indeed," came the reply. "The prophet Micah tells us this:

'Bethlehem in the land of Judah,
　　you are by no means the least of the leading cities of Judah;
for from you will come a leader
　　who will guide my people Israel.' "

Matthew 2:6 [Micah 5:2]

So Herod called the men from the East to a secret meeting. He asked them to tell him all about the star, and when it had first appeared. Then he sent them to Bethlehem. "Search for the king," he said. "When you find him, tell me where he is, so that I, too, may go and worship him."

Then Herod sent the travellers on their way and sat alone with his dark, tormenting fears.

The Wise Men Find Jesus

The travellers set out for Bethlehem, as they had been advised.

"Look," said one. "There is the star we first saw in the east."

"It lights the path we are now taking," said another.

"We must certainly be going the right way," said the third.

And they laughed together, delighted that their quest was proving so successful.

The star went ahead of them to Bethlehem and stopped over one of the houses there.

Inside, they found the child they sought, with his mother, Mary.

They knelt down and worshipped him, and gave him the gifts they had brought: gold, frankincense, and myrrh.

Then they returned to their own country. But, from a dream, they learned that it would not be wise to return to Jerusalem, to Herod, so they chose a different road.

The Escape to Egypt

After the men from the East had left, Joseph had another dream in which an angel spoke to him. "Herod will be looking for the child," warned the angel. "Get up now, take Mary and the baby with you, and escape while you can. Go to Egypt, where Herod will not find you. Stay there until I tell you to leave."

Joseph did as the angel said.

Herod soon discovered that the men from the East had tricked him, but he could not forget that a child who might claim kingship had been born. So he sent soldiers down to Bethlehem.

"Seek out all the boys who are two years old or younger," he commanded, "and kill them."

The terrible orders were carried out, and the land was filled with weeping.

The Story of the Boy Jesus

*Little is known about Jesus' boyhood, but the Bible
tells one story of the time when he was twelve years old.*

❧

Mary and her son, Jesus, stood in the shade of an olive tree and gazed
across the valley toward Jerusalem and its splendid Temple, gleaming
white and gold.

The place where it stood was the place where the nation's wise King Solomon
had built the first Temple, the place where a struggling band of pioneers had
rebuilt a temple after they returned from exile in Babylon. But this building was
the work of King Herod—the one who had massacred the children of Bethlehem
when he heard that a new king had been born.

Jesus was twelve now, and for all anyone knew he was simply a good son to
her and Joseph. They had returned from Egypt to their home in Nazareth as
soon as they heard that Herod had died. Jesus had grown up in the little town
just like any other boy. He was a thoughtful child. He loved to go to the school
run by the rabbi at the little synagogue. He had been so eager to learn and
worked hard to be able to read from the precious scrolls where the law of Moses
and the sayings of the prophets were written.

Now he was almost a man and had come with a group of pilgrims from
Nazareth to celebrate the festival of the Passover at the Temple.

The week of celebrations passed. When it was time to return home, all the
young boys seemed to have grown suddenly to manhood and shuffled along in
a group together, some way off behind their parents.

That evening, Mary and Joseph waited for Jesus to join them. He didn't
come. Joseph asked the other boys where he was, but they shrugged and said
they hadn't seen him all day. As the sun sank low in the sky, Mary realized with
a sudden lurch of panic that Jesus was missing. He wasn't anywhere among the
group.

"He's only a boy," she wept, and she and her husband hurried back to the
city. "He could have gone off with anyone . . . or they could have gone off with
him." For three long days, they searched the city. Mary was pale with anxiety.

"Let's go to the Temple," her husband suggested. "We can at least pray for
Jesus there."

There, in the courtyard, they found Jesus. He was sitting talking with the most
learned rabbis about the Law and the prophets and what they understood about
God. The rabbis were nodding, clearly impressed with the way he spoke.

"How could you put me through such misery?" Mary rushed into the middle of them, with rage and relief. "We have been so worried about you!"

Jesus looked up with the confidence of a young man. "Why did you have to look for me?" he asked. "Didn't you know that I had to be in my Father's house?" Mary and Joseph did not understand him, but Jesus returned to Nazareth with them, as an obedient son.

The Story of John

Jesus had a cousin, John. An angel had told of his birth and had told John's father that the child was to be dedicated to God. When John grew up, he lived like a prophet of old, preaching in the wilderness.

❧

Walking to and from the well to collect water was always a challenge, thought Mary to herself. It wasn't the weight of the water; it was the gossip and the nastiness of the conversations.

"Your nephew John is quite a character, I hear," called out one woman, a notorious chatterbox. "A wilderness prophet with wild hair and rough old clothes. I wonder what his parents, Elizabeth and Zechariah, would have thought."

"They adored everything about him," Mary replied confidently. "And here in Nazareth we should all be grateful to him."

"Why is that?" chimed in another.

Mary smiled. "Haven't you noticed that your tax payments have been reduced?" she said. "Our local tax collector went to hear John speak, and he came back quite repentant. John told him to charge no more than is legal . . . and that's what he's doing. He even let John baptize him in the Jordan in front of a whole crowd of people from whom he collects taxes. As baptism means a new start, he couldn't easily go back on his promise."

"My daughter has become all enthusiastic about good works, too," confessed another woman. "She used to work so hard making fancy clothes for herself. Now she's making clothes for the family down the street who are less fortunate. John's teachings made a big impression on her."

"And they say that John is going around announcing the coming of God's Messiah, the one the prophets spoke of." All the women were fascinated by this news, and they went home chattering enthusiastically about what the Messiah would be like.

That evening, when the day's work was done, Mary told Jesus of the conversations she had been having. She wasn't surprised at Jesus' reply.

"I'm going to go and visit John myself," he announced. "Now is the right time for me to take a new path."

When Jesus reached the place down by the Jordan where John was preaching, a crowd was already gathered.

"There is one coming after me who is greater than I am." John's words echoed off the rocky cliffs nearby. "I'm not good enough even to untie his sandals."

As John spoke about the Messiah he believed was coming, Jesus made his way through the crowd. When John had finished speaking, Jesus asked to be baptized.

John looked at his cousin, and he knew for sure what lay ahead for Jesus. "No," he whispered. "You should be baptizing me."

"Let it be as I ask for now," replied Jesus. "In this way, we will do what God requires."

So John baptized Jesus in the River Jordan. As he lifted Jesus out of the water, the spirit of God came down on Jesus like a dove and a voice from heaven spoke:

"You are my own dear Son. I am pleased with you."

Luke 3:22

The Story of Jesus the Teacher

*Jesus had been baptized by John. As he had been lifted up out of the
River Jordan, he knew that he was embarking on a new path in life.*

❦

Jesus' new path took him first out into the dry and dusty desert, where birds
of prey hovered above the weird, wind-sculpted rocks and fierce animals
slumbered in caves till the chill winds of evening stirred.

For forty days, Jesus stayed in the wilderness, eating nothing and thinking only
of the life that lay ahead of him.

"It doesn't have to be like this." The thought whispered in Jesus' ear like the
rustle of dry leaves in the wind. "It's your life, and you can choose how to live it."

Jesus stared idly at the landscape, where a pile of rocks had crumbled at the
foot of a cliff.

"And you're so hungry," came the thought. "If every one of those stones was
a piece of bread, you could eat it."

Jesus looked again, knowing that God could work miracles.

"Go on," said the thought. "If you are God's Son, order this stone to turn
into bread."

"No!" Jesus was alert again. "The scriptures say, 'Man cannot live by bread
alone.' "

The whisper floated away on the breeze. Jesus got up and walked briskly. He
came to the top of a cliff.

"Imagine." It was the whisper again. "You're the king on the mountain. Below
lie all the kingdoms of the world. And they're mine to give to anyone I choose . . .
all that power and wealth . . . if you worship me."

Jesus knew for certain who the whisper was, and he answered the devil once
more. "The scriptures say, 'Worship the Lord your God, and serve only him!' "

There came eerie laughter . . . a jackal, perhaps, or something more menacing.

Jesus walked on over the ridges. He remembered, as a boy, walking to Jerusalem
and suddenly seeing the Temple before him, towering over all the city.

"Can you see yourself on the highest point of the Temple?" came the whisper.
"There you are . . . and all the people of Jerusalem craning their necks to see you
boldly standing there. If you are God's Son, throw yourself down. You know the
scriptures; they say this: 'God will order his angels to take good care of you.' "

Jesus laughed aloud. "Go away, Satan!" he ordered. "The scriptures also say,
'Do not put the Lord your God to the test.' "

The whisper hurried away in an angry swirl of dust.

Water and Wine

Mary was enjoying the wedding more than any other she had been to in years. The bridegroom was being very generous. He had invited as many people as he could. As a result, not only was she one of the guests, along with her son, Jesus, but the host had also invited Jesus' closest disciples—a merry band of fishermen and others whom he had invited to join him in his new walk of life. . . . And there were people Mary knew from the surrounding villages whom she hadn't seen in years.

"Is it true that Jesus was thrown out of the synagogue in Nazareth?" It was an acquaintance from another village who spoke.

"I know there was some trouble when he read from the scriptures recently and they didn't like what he said about them," replied Mary. "But Jesus has decided to live in Capernaum, on Lake Galilee. Some of his best friends live there."

"He's beginning to get a lot of attention wherever he goes, isn't he?" the friend persisted. "People are beginning to whisper that he might be the nation's Messiah."

Mary nodded. "I've heard it said," she replied disinterestedly.

"Isn't that what his little remark in the synagogue hinted at?"

Mary shrugged, and the acquaintance left, clearly disappointed at not wheedling out more gossip. It was hard work, sometimes, being the mother of Jesus. She looked at her son, laughing and drinking, and wondered if he knew what she had to endure.

"OOOH, dear!" A young man's voice boomed out. "Not much wine left in this jug. Can you get some more?" He waved the jug at a servant.

But just then the bridegroom's mother came running forward. "I'll take care of that," she cried.

The woman took the jug and sank onto a cushion next to Mary. "My son has been too generous with his invitations," she sobbed. "We have no more wine. He will be so embarrassed. And he wanted this to be the best party ever."

Mary put a hand on the woman's shoulder. "Wait a moment," she said. "I have an idea."

She marched up to Jesus. "They have no wine left," she whispered. Then she gave him the kind of reproachful look she used to give when he was little.

"You mustn't tell me what to do," replied Jesus firmly. "My time hasn't come."

But Mary sauntered off. She whispered something to the servants, and they came right over to Jesus.

Jesus looked around. There were some huge water jars close by. "Fill them with water," he said.

Then he said to the servants, "Now draw off some of the water, and take it to the man in charge of the feast."

They did so. The man took the cup, tasted the contents, and beamed. "Wonderful!" he called to the bridegroom. "Everyone I know serves their best wine first, and keeps the poorer stuff till later. But you have saved the best till now."

The Two House Builders

News of Jesus spread throughout the region of Galilee. "He can heal people with a touch," it was said. So those who were ill were brought to him, and many were made well.

Jesus became known as a teacher, and he spoke to the crowds about how to live in a way that pleases God: "Love your enemies, do good to those who hate you, bless those who curse you, and pray for those who ill-treat you. . . . Give to everyone who asks you for something, and when someone takes what is yours, do not ask for it back. Do for others just what you want them to do for you."

Among the crowds were people Jesus had known all his life, and they laughed and joked.

"Oh, yes, Lord," guffawed a group of young men.

"We obey!" hooted others.

Jesus grinned. These were men he had worked alongside in his days on the local building sites.

"Do not flock to me, calling me 'Lord, Lord,' if you do not do what I tell you," he shouted.

The men came nearer. "We don't understand your clever words," they said. "Make it simple for your old friends."

"It's like this. . . ." replied Jesus. "Anyone who comes to me and listens to my words and obeys them is like a master builder, someone who takes the time to select the right place on which to build, on solid ground, high above the flood plain. There, he digs good foundations. He chooses good quality materials—well-cut stone, solid timber—and he is careful to build straight and true. It takes time, and it takes effort, but it is worth it. When the rains come, the river rises suddenly and overflows its banks, but his house is safe, and neither flood nor winds can destroy it.

"But what of the person who hears my words and does not obey them? That person is like the kind of builder you wouldn't want to know! There's land down on the flood plain that's cheap and easy to get hold of. It's a light sand in which it's easy to dig a shallow foundation and construct an attractive-looking building in no time. But when the rains pour down and the rivers overflow and the wind blows with all its might, the house falls with a terrible crash!"

The Prayer

Jesus and his disciples were walking out of town. As they turned a corner, they came upon a small group of men with shawls covering their heads and hands lifted—they were praying in the traditional manner.

"Excuse me," said Peter teasingly, as he stepped around them. The men went on praying, but the showy way they lifted their arms a little higher was a sure sign—they were delighted to have been noticed.

"I hope you don't want us to get religious like that," muttered John to Jesus.

"Certainly not," came the reply. "When you pray, go somewhere peaceful, where you can be alone. Go into your room and close the door. God, your Father, who sees what you do in private, will reward you."

The group walked off into the hills. There, Jesus wandered off to be by himself. The disciples knew he would be praying in some quiet place and did not try to follow him.

"What do you think he says, when he spends time in prayer?" asked one.

"No idea," replied another. "I run out of things to say almost before I've begun. John used to teach his disciples what to say in their prayers. I wish Jesus would."

"Here's Jesus now," called another. "Let's ask him."

Jesus gave them this prayer:

"Our Father in heaven:
may your name be held holy,
your kingdom come,
your will be done,
on earth as in heaven.
Give us today our daily bread.
And forgive us our wrongdoing,
as we have forgiven those who have done wrong to us.
And do not put us to the test,
but save us from the evil one."

Matthew 6:9–13

179

Wind and Waves

One evening, after another long day spent talking to the crowds, Jesus sat wearily in the boat they used to travel to the lakeside communities.

"Let's go to the other side," he suggested.

Among the disciples were a number who had been fishermen. They took charge of the sail and steered the boat out into the middle of the lake. Jesus fell asleep.

"It's quiet, isn't it?" said Peter. There was no noise other than the gentle swish of water cresting past the bow as the boat glided on its way and a faint creak of the timbers.

John looked around him. "Strangely so," he replied. He paused a moment. "I'm just hoping it's not the calm before the storm."

Peter nodded. He adjusted the sail and headed for the shore that seemed nearest.

The canvas flapped and then began to flutter noisily. "Watch out!" called John. "All hands at the ready."

With a sudden, angry howl, the wind blew down from the hills, bringing with it a legion of jagged, tattered clouds swooping through the night sky. The waters heaved and rose, and fearsome waves began to crash against the boat and over the sides.

Matthew had been a tax collector and was not used to sailing. He gripped the boat in terror. "Is this normal?" he shouted.

"No it isn't," Peter shouted back. "Grab a bucket and get some of that water out. Now. Fast!"

Matthew worked as hard as he could, fear lending him a strength he didn't know he had. Then he saw Jesus still sleeping. "Wake up, wake up!" he called. "Don't you care that we're about to die?"

A sudden wave threw everyone to the floor of the boat. Jesus picked himself up and looked around.

"Be quiet," he said to the waves. "Be still," he said to the winds.

At once there was calm. "Why are you frightened?" he asked. "Have you no faith?"

The men were stunned and silent. Who is this man? they wondered. Even the wind and waves obey him.

The Beloved Daughter

"Where's Father gone? He promised to stay with me."

The girl looked forlornly into her mother's eyes. She felt very ill. She wanted both her parents to be there at her bedside.

"He's gone to get help," comforted the mother. "He'll return as quickly as he can."

As quickly as I can, Jairus was thinking to himself. I must get back to my daughter as quickly as I can. But I can hardly move through this crowd.

He was squeezing himself through a great crush of people who had gathered on the lakeshore to see Jesus. Some of the people recognized him and let him pass, for he was an official at the local synagogue; others had come from goodness knows where, and they stood firm, elbowing him aside without a glance.

"Please, please let me through. My daughter is dying. I need to see Jesus." Tears were streaming down Jairus' face. Then suddenly he was there, right at Jesus' feet. Jairus fell to his knees. "Please help me," he wept. "My only daughter is dying . . . and she's just twelve. Please can you heal her?"

Jesus smiled and nodded, but Jairus found it almost impossible to lead him anywhere through the jostling crowd, where grown-ups tugged at both of them, and children reached out to touch the man who, it was said, could work miracles.

Then, all at once, Jesus stopped. "Someone touched me," he said. "Who was it?"

His look was sharp and piercing, and, for a moment, the crowds stepped back, shaking their heads. One of his disciples, Peter, simply laughed. "There are crowds around you, Jesus," he said. "It could have been anyone."

"When I was touched, power went out from me," Jesus said. Then one woman stepped forward and bent low. "I have been suffering for twelve years," she murmured, "but when I touched the edge of your cloak, I was well again."

Jesus smiled. "Your faith has made you well. Go in peace," he said.

"And now, let us hurry," urged Jesus. As Jairus turned to lead Jesus to his home, a servant arrived. "Your daughter has died," he said. "The Teacher doesn't need to come now."

Jairus began to sob, but Jesus simply put a hand on his shoulder. "Don't be afraid," he said. "Only believe, and she will be well."

When they reached Jairus' house, the mourners had already arrived and were wailing noisily to make known the grief of those who wept within.

Jesus sent them away and went into the house with the girl's father and three of his disciples. He took the girl's limp hand. "Get up, my child!" he said.

She blinked her eyes and sat up, and said, "Father's back. And I'm really hungry."

"Give her something to eat," said Jesus.

The Miraculous Food

Out on the hillside, Jesus spoke to the crowds through the long, hot day.

When the sun was beginning to set, Jesus' twelve disciples came up to him and said, "It's time to send the people away. They will need to find food and a place to stay the night in the surrounding farms and villages."

"You feed them," said Jesus.

"What with?" they asked. "It would cost a fortune to feed this many people—there must be a few thousand here."

"Don't worry," joked another. "There's a boy here with five round breads and two fish. That should do!" Everyone laughed.

Jesus took the food. "All right," he said. "Get everyone to sit down in groups of about fifty." They did so.

Then Jesus took the bread and the fish, looked to heaven and gave thanks to God for the food.

Next, he broke the food into pieces and asked the disciples to hand out some to each of the groups.

"Listen," said John to his group of people. "Here are two pieces of bread and a fish you can divide up. Take a piece and pass it on."

"Here we go," said the first person to the next. I've taken some and there's still more for you.

Then that person explained to the next, "I took quite a chunk of bread but not so much fish. There seems to be plenty of both."

So the conversations went on. The food was passed from one to another. Everyone took what they wanted, and there was always something to pass on. Soon, everyone was eating contentedly.

"Gather up the scraps," Jesus urged his disciples. "We want to leave these hills as calm and peaceful as we found them."

The men set to work. "Here's a piece of bread," murmured John to himself, "and another and another . . ." He stood up straight and looked around. All the disciples were hard at work, their baskets filling rapidly. How can there be more leftovers than there was food to start with? he wondered.

At the end of the day, there were twelve baskets of scraps.

The Lost Sheep

Among the people who gathered to see Jesus were those who were very religious.

"As a teacher of the Law," said one, "I am very concerned to make sure that this wandering preacher is not leading the people astray with what he says."

"As a Pharisee," added another, "I am worried that he doesn't teach the importance of a pure and holy life."

They all looked to where Jesus was sitting. On this occasion, he was surrounded by a motley array of beggars, vagrants, and people who were suspected of criminal dealing and terrorism.

Jesus waved them over. They stepped forward but then had to wait as a shepherd led his sheep along the path that lay between them, ambling slowly forward so the animals that straggled behind could catch up.

"Just think about shepherds and how they go about their work," said Jesus when they arrived. "Imagine——a shepherd has one hundred sheep. He is leading them along, but when he turns and counts them, he finds that one is missing. What does he do? He leaves the ninety-nine grazing in the pasture and goes looking for the one that is lost.

"And what does he do when at last he finds it? Does he beat it and punish it till it bleats in terror and pain? Of course not! It is his treasure, and he is delighted to find it. So he picks it up and lays it across his shoulders so he can carry it home.

"Then, when it is safely home, he calls to all his friends, 'Today is my happy day. I found my lost sheep. Let us celebrate together!'

"I tell you," said Jesus, "there is more rejoicing in heaven over one sinner who repents of their ways than over ninety-nine respectable people who do not need to repent."

The Parable of the Good Samaritan

One day, as Jesus was sitting with his disciples, a teacher of the Law approached. He smiled a broad smile—the sort of smile that is hard to trust.

"Ah, Teacher," he said to Jesus, bowing a little too low. Jesus raised his eyebrows. "There is one question that has been puzzling me dreadfully, and after hearing so much from everyone about what a wise person you are, I thought I'd ask you. What must I do to receive eternal life?"

"What do the scriptures say?" Jesus answered.

The man replied, " 'Love the Lord your God with all your heart, with all your soul, with all your strength, and with all your mind' and 'Love your fellow human beings as you love yourself.' "

"You are right," replied Jesus. "Do this and you will live." And he smiled at the man.

The teacher wasn't going to be dismissed that easily. "Whom should I consider my fellow human beings?" he asked.

Jesus replied, "Once upon a time, there was a man travelling from Jerusalem to Jericho . . . a lonely road, if ever there was one. As he travelled, he was attacked by bandits. They snatched his purse, beat him up, took all he had, and left him for dead."

"I'm entirely with you in condemning the criminal element in society," interrupted the man. Jesus seemed not to notice.

"It just so happened that a priest was going that way," Jesus continued. "He saw the man, but walked by on the other side."

"Isn't it hard to know what to do when you find yourself at the scene of a crime," the teacher commented.

"Next," said Jesus, "came a Levite. He went over to look, then hurried away."

"A real dilemma for a Levite." The man certainly liked to talk. "After all, he couldn't risk touching a dead body if he was on the way to the Temple, because that would have made him unfit to carry out his duties on account of the Law that says . . ."

One of the disciples yawned, and Jesus started talking again. "A Samaritan was also travelling that way . . ."

"Don't you just wish that Samaritans would stay in Samaria with their own strange, regional ways and leave us alone?" added the man.

"And," said Jesus, "he saw the man and felt sorry for him. He tended the man's wounds, lifted him onto his donkey, and took him to an inn. He paid the innkeeper to take care of him, promising to return and pay any extra that might be needed."

Then Jesus asked, "Which of the three treated the man who was robbed as he himself would have liked to have been treated?"

"The one who was kind to him," sulked the man.

"You go and do the same," said Jesus.

The Prodigal Son

Jesus told this story:

"There was once a man who had two sons. They worked together on the land and made a good living. As he grew up, the younger son began to dream of what he would do if he had his father's riches, and then he made a plan.

" 'Father,' he announced one day, 'when you die, I will inherit some of your wealth. I want to have it now, while I am young.'

" 'My dear son, I fear you are making a mistake,' pleaded the father. But it was no use. Sorrowfully, his father divided his property between his two sons.

"Within days, the son sold it and set off for a country far away. There he found much on which to spend his money, with extravagant lodgings and stylish clothes and rich food. Friends gathered around him, eager to come to his parties. He was delighted. But his money soon dwindled away.

"Then, out of nowhere, famine struck the land and the price of everything soared. With nothing left to sell, the young man became desperate.

"He found himself a job . . . but it was of the very worst kind, looking after pigs. He carried a basketful of bean pods to the field they had rooted into dust and tipped the food on the ground in front of them. I wish I could eat bean pods, he thought, as he watched them munching. No one gives me anything.

"He began to think of the family farm and the servants who had looked after the flocks. 'They always had more than enough to eat,' he remembered. Then he lifted his head. 'I shall go back to my father,' he said, 'and admit that I have done wrong.'

"So he made the long journey home. But while he was still a long way off, his father saw him. He ran to greet him and kissed him. The son hung his head. 'Father, I have sinned against God and against you. I am no longer fit to be called your son. Treat me as one of your hired workers.'

"His father simply waved his hand. 'Hurry!' he called to the servants. 'Bring a robe for my son, a ring for his finger, and shoes for his feet. Then let us prepare a feast.'

"So it was done. The party began, and the elder son returned from the fields to hear music and dancing. 'What's going on?' he asked a servant.

" 'Your brother has come back,' he was told. 'Your father has prepared a feast to celebrate.'

"At that, the elder brother grew so angry he would not even go into the house. His father came out to welcome him in.

" 'I have worked for you all these years and yet you have done nothing for me!' the son complained.

"The father replied, 'You are always here with me, and everything I have is yours. But we had to celebrate and be happy—your brother was dead, but now he is alive; he was lost, but now he has been found.' "

Jesus and the Children

Jesus was sitting by himself, waiting for his disciples to join him. He heard the sound of footsteps.

He turned. Coming toward him, with anxious smiles, was a group of mothers. At their heels were a dozen or more children: some trying to look grand and solemn, others dodging behind one another so as not to be seen. They all looked amazingly well scrubbed, with their hair neatly combed. Their mothers had clearly been busy getting them ready.

One little girl darted forward. "Are you the miracle worker?" she asked with sudden boldness. Jesus laughed, as a mother rushed forward to hush her daughter.

Then the mother herself looked a little bashful. "We have come to ask if you will just . . . give a little blessing to each of our children. People say that you are the . . . the One. . . ." She ran out of words.

"We feel that your blessing will be really important," another chimed in, "because it's clear from all you say and do that you have been chosen by God for something special."

Jesus reached out his hands to welcome each child, but just then his disciples returned.

"Please don't bother the Teacher," one called out stridently. "He's always busy; he needs some time to himself."

"If you don't mind, it would be best if you went home now," another added, a bit more gently.

The mothers looked embarrassed. The children looked up in confusion. "Have we done something wrong?" asked one, her eyes filling with tears.

"Leave them alone." It was Jesus who spoke, and he was talking to his disciples. "Let the children come to me and do not stop them, because the kingdom of God belongs to little ones like these. Remember this! Whoever does not receive the kingdom of God like a child will never enter it."

The Story of Jesus in Jerusalem

For three years, Jesus travelled the land, telling stories, working miracles, and teaching people about God. Then, one spring, he and his disciples set off for Jerusalem.

❦

Jesus and his band of disciples were travelling to Jerusalem to celebrate the Passover festival there. At the Mount of Olives he stopped. Over the valley was Mount Zion itself, where Jerusalem's beautiful Temple stood. He spoke to two of his friends. "Go to the village ahead," he said. "You will find a donkey tethered with her colt beside her. Bring the animals here. If anyone questions you, say, 'The Master needs them.' "

So they did, and Jesus settled himself on a colt that had never been ridden before. His friends watched and some remembered that in the scriptures it was written:

"Shout for joy, you people of Jerusalem!
Look, your king is coming to you!
He comes triumphant and victorious,
    but humble and riding on a donkey—
    on a colt, the foal of a donkey."

Zechariah 9:9–10

Jesus urged the donkey forward on the steep road down into the valley. Many people were travelling to Jerusalem for the festival, and they began to talk.

"Look! Some people are beginning to lay their cloaks on the ground in front of him. Let's go closer! They're giving him a hero's welcome."

It was true. The whispering and the gossiping turned to cheering and shouting. Some people cut branches from the palm trees by the side of the road and waved them.

"Praise to the son of our great King David!"

"God bless the king who comes in the name of the Lord!"

Children jostled and women danced; men shouted and punched their fists in the air, for surely this Jesus was coming to the city to lead his people against the Romans. Perhaps this was the start of an uprising? The beginning of a new era of freedom?

Among the crowd were some religious leaders, who were suspicious of this upstart teacher and his so-called miracles. They elbowed their way to the front.

"Teacher," they said angrily, "command your followers to be quiet."

The little donkey plodded gently on over the carpet of cloaks. Jesus smiled calmly at the men who now tugged at the donkey's bridle, vainly trying to make it stop.

"Even if the people keep quiet," said Jesus, "the very stones will start shouting."

And he went on his journey, up the winding path and through the gate that led to the Temple itself.

Jesus and the Temple Merchants

As the time of the Passover festival approached, the Temple courtyard was busier than ever. Money changers rubbed their hands with glee as pilgrims arrived from all over the world to be in Jerusalem for the celebration. There were Temple taxes to be paid, and for this they needed to exchange some of their own money for Temple coins . . . and in the exchange, the merchants made a profit.

Above the hubbub of bargaining came the sound of sheep bleating and cattle bellowing in fear. "Perfect animals for sacrifice!" called the merchants, and "You would expect to pay a high price for beasts of this quality," they said haughtily to would-be purchasers.

Some of the Temple visitors were wealthy, idly paying whatever price they were asked with no worries and lavishly pouring coins into the Temple treasury. Others were poor, desperately trying to haggle a fairer price and counting out the little they had.

This was the scene that greeted Jesus as he arrived with his disciples. For a while, he stood, silent and grim. Then he motioned to one of his friends to bring him a bag they had brought with them. He rummaged inside and pulled out some cord, which he began to twist and knot.

A minute later, he stood up and shook the little whip he had made. Then he delivered a smart smack to the rump of a calf that stood close by.

The animal kicked out and hit another. Jesus moved down the line of animals, flicking the whip.

"Out, out!" called Jesus, driving the animals to the gateway.

"What do you think you're doing?" called a merchant . . . but too late. The animals stampeded, scattering the pilgrims and knocking over tables. Coins rolled away and settled in the cracks between the stones, and children scrabbled eagerly to pick them up.

Officials raced to find the cause of the hubbub . . . and there was Jesus, purposefully tipping over a table that was piled high with coins. "This has nothing to do with the worship of God!" he was shouting at the enraged owner. "Get out, you thief. Stop making it a marketplace."

The official pinned Jesus to the wall with his finger. "How dare you?" he seethed. "What miracle can you perform to justify what you have done?"

Jesus replied, "Tear this Temple down, and I'll build it up again in three days."

"What do you mean?" stormed the man. "It's you who's tearing things down, not me."

"The man's mad," said a second official. "This reckless deed just confirms the worst of all I've heard about him."

The first one shook his head. "He's dangerous, too. And he'll pay for it."

Jesus' enemies began getting ready for action.

Jesus and the Great Commandment

At Passover time, Jesus and his disciples gathered for a meal.

The room was filled with their talk: some laughing, some arguing mildly, others in earnest debate with one another.

And there was Judas Iscariot—silent, watchful, secretive.

Sighing deeply, Jesus got up from the table and took off his outer tunic. He tied a towel around his waist and poured some water into a basin.

The disciples watched, curious. What on earth was their master doing?

Quietly, Jesus moved among them, performing the everyday, humble task of washing their dusty feet and drying them with the towel . . . the job of a household servant.

"Are you going to wash my feet, Lord?" It was Peter, always the loudmouth, always bold enough to question whatever he saw.

"You do not understand what I am doing now," replied Jesus, "but you will understand later."

"Never will I let you wash my feet," declared Peter. "It's not right for you to do that."

"If I don't," replied Jesus, "then you will no longer be my disciple."

Peter was too enthusiastic a follower to allow that. "In that case," he said, "wash my feet, and my hands, and my head."

But Jesus refused. "Only your feet need washing," he insisted.

When the task was completed, Jesus returned to his place. "Do you understand what I have done?" he asked. "You call me 'Teacher' and 'Lord,' and that is what I am among you. But I have washed your feet. You should wash one another's feet."

The talking resumed. Then Jesus took a piece of bread, gave thanks to God, broke it, and gave it to his disciples, saying, "This is my body, which is given for you. Do this in memory of me." In the same way, he gave them the cup after the supper, saying, "This cup is God's new covenant sealed with my blood, which is poured out for you."

Some time later, without a word, Judas left, and the disciples all thought he must be on some errand only he and Jesus knew of.

"I won't be with you much longer," said Jesus heavily, looking around the table. "But there is something I want you to remember always. I am going to give you a new commandment. Love one another. As I have loved you, so you must love one another. If you have love for one another, people will know you are my disciples."

The Betrayal

Jesus and his disciples fell to talking about what lay ahead of them now that their enemies were ready for action.

"One thing you can be sure of," said Peter to Jesus. "I'm your loyal disciple. If you go to prison, I go to prison. If you die, I die."

"Don't be so sure," warned Jesus. "Before the cock crows at dawn, you will have said three times that you do not know me."

They all went out into the dark night. Jesus wanted to spend some time in the olive grove on the opposite side of the valley, in the Garden of Gethsemane. He went a short distance away from his disciples and prayed. What was going to happen to him now that his enemies were gathering?

"Father," he said, "take this cup of suffering away from me. Not my will, however, but your will be done."

In his heart, he knew that he must face the torment to come, and he prayed all the more, weeping as he did so.

The hours passed; the disciples simply slept.

Then came a shout, the sound of scuffling feet. Judas Iscariot stepped forward and kissed Jesus; then armed men came out from the shadows and arrested him.

The disciples were ready to fight, but Jesus would not let them. He allowed himself to be taken to the house of the High Priest, and Peter followed.

As the door slammed on Jesus and the guard, Peter sat with the soldiers and servants who were milling around in the courtyard, and warmed himself by the fire. The night wore on. Peter grew anxious and sullen.

"Hey, I know you," said a servant girl, who joined the group. "You're one of Jesus' followers."

A soldier gripped his sword. Peter looked startled. "I don't even know him," he stuttered.

Later a man came along. "You're one of Jesus' followers, aren't you?" he said.

"No, I'm not," snarled Peter.

An hour went by. The sky paled. Peter was dragged into conversation with some servants.

"I can tell by your accent that you're from Galilee," said a man passing by. "In fact," he said, peering more closely, "you're one of Jesus' disciples."

"I don't know what you're talking about," cursed Peter.

It was then that Jesus was hustled out. Peter stood up. A cock crowed. Then Jesus turned and looked straight at Peter.

And Peter wept.

The Story of the Crucifixion

The people who hated Jesus had finally trapped him. They began to scheme for him to be put to death. Then, they believed, his followers would be scattered and his teachings forgotten.

❧

Jesus was on trial before the elders of his own people—the chief priests and the teachers of the Law.

"Are you the Messiah?" they demanded to know.

Jesus would not give a clear yes or a clear no. Whispering together, the elders made plans about what to do next, and hustled him off to stand trial before the Roman governor Pontius Pilate.

"This man has been misleading our people," they told Pilate. "He has been telling them not to pay taxes to the Roman emperor. He claims that he is our people's Messiah, which of course means he is setting himself up as our king." They smiled—the Roman governor would surely not dare to put up with anyone who threatened his rule.

So Jesus was questioned over and over again. I can find nothing against this man, Pilate mused. It must be that these people are getting uptight for reasons of tradition. I will have the man whipped and let him go.

When the elders of Jesus' people heard Pilate's ruling, they were dismayed. "The crowd will not accept your decision," they warned. "Just ask them."

Below the place where Pilate sat in judgment a crowd had gathered. It was the custom that the governor would show mercy and release a prisoner at Passover time. Jesus' enemies had done their work well. "Free Barabbas!" the crowd cried. Barabbas was in prison for causing a riot and for murder.

Pilate was taken aback. "But what about this man?" Pilate asked, indicating Jesus. "He has done no wrong."

"Crucify him! Crucify him!" they cried. Pilate pleaded in vain. "Crucify, crucify!" they chanted. The mood was growing angry, and Pilate began to fear a riot.

"Very well, then," he agreed. He took some water and washed his hands in front of them. "I am not responsible for the death of this man," he announced. "It is your doing."

Soldiers led Jesus away, along with two thieves who had been condemned to death. On a hillside just outside the city, the grisly work of nailing each of them to a cross of wood was carried out as the heat rose in the late morning.

Jesus' mother watched his agony, and stood in tears looking up at her son . . . the baby in the manger, the boy in the Temple, the young man at the wedding, the teacher surrounded by adoring crowds. Jesus saw her, and he saw his disciple John. "There is your son now," he said to Mary; to his friend he said, "There is your mother."

Around noon, the sun stopped shining, and darkness covered the whole country for three long hours.

Suddenly, Jesus cried out, "My God, my God, why did you abandon me?" Then his head slumped forward, and he died.

The Tomb

Jesus hung dead upon the cross.

One of his secret followers was a wealthy man named Joseph, from the town of Arimathea. He made an agreement with Pilate that he would arrange for the body to be buried.

As the sun sank low in the sky, a small group of women watched as Jesus' body was wrapped in a linen cloth and taken to a tomb cut into the rock of a nearby olive grove.

"What of the proper burial traditions?" they asked anxiously, for they wanted to do all they could for their friend and teacher.

"They will have to wait," answered Joseph grimly. "Our sabbath day of rest is beginning. Stand back, and let us roll the stone door in place." They pushed the round stone along the groove in the rock that guided it firmly over the entrance to the cave.

The sabbath passed. Just as the next day's dawn was breaking, the women returned with spices to anoint the body in the proper fashion. "Who will roll away the door for us?" they asked anxiously. "It was a very large stone— remember how the men struggled to push it into place?"

They looked ahead, peering through the shadows of the dawn light toward the rocks and trees silhouetted against the paling sky.

"What has happened?" gasped the one named Mary Magdalene. "The door is open."

Fear flooded through them, slowing their steps. "Let's go in," said Salome. "Perhaps Joseph or his servants has come ahead of us to complete the burial."

So they entered the tomb. "The body has gone," whispered Mary in alarm. She looked around more closely, then shrieked in fright. A young man was sitting on the ledge to the right. He was wearing a white robe.

"Don't be alarmed," he said gently. "I know you are looking for Jesus of Nazareth, who was crucified. He is not here—he is risen from the dead. Now go and give this message to the disciples, including Peter: 'Jesus is going into Galilee ahead of you. There you will see him, just as he told you.' "

The women fled. "Can it possibly be true?" said Salome to her companion.

"Try to remember exactly what Jesus said," replied Mary. "He did talk about dying . . . and no one wanted to believe him."

Salome replied, "This is what Peter told me. I learned it word for word. He said: 'The Son of Man must suffer much and be rejected by the elders, the chief priests, and the teachers of the Law. He will be put to death, but three days later he will rise to life.' It's impossible, though, isn't it?" she said sadly.

The Story of the Resurrection

The tomb was empty. What could possibly have happened? Where was Jesus?

❧

Mary Magdalene stood and wept. Beyond the olive trees, the sky turned to gold as the sun rose above the hills. A bird sang. A gentle breeze rustled the leaves.

If I look again in the tomb, she thought to herself, perhaps it will all be different. Perhaps the body of Jesus will still be there. Then we will at least be able to complete the burial and say our good-byes.

She stooped down by the entrance. A ray of sunlight darted in, and there were two angels sitting in the very place where the body of Jesus had been. They smiled at her. "Woman, why are you crying?" they asked.

Hardly believing what she saw, she heard herself reply, "They have taken the body of my Lord, and I do not know where they have put him."

A shadow fell, and Mary turned around. A man was standing there, looking at her with concern. "Woman, why are you crying," he asked her.

At least this is real, she thought to herself. The day is beginning, and this must be the man who tends the olive grove.

"Sir, if you are the one who took him away, please tell me where you put him, so I can go and get him," she stammered.

The man bent closer, smiling gently. "Mary," he said.

She gasped. "Teacher!" she whispered in wonder, and she reached out her hands.

The man stood up again. "Do not hold on to me," Jesus told her, "because I have not yet gone back up to the Father. But go to my brothers and tell them that I am returning to him who is my Father and their Father, who is my God and their God."

So Mary went and told the disciples that she had seen the Lord.

Doubting Thomas

The evening sun was going down, and the disciples were in complete confusion. The stories they had heard through the day had unsettled them completely.

"This is my version of what happened," said John. "Mary Magdalene came at dawn and told us she'd been to the tomb, and that our master's body had gone. I ran there as fast as I could, and when I peered in, I just saw the linen grave cloths, nothing else."

"Then I came along," added Peter, "and I went straight in. There was nothing there except the grave cloths."

"Nothing," added John.

"For goodness' sake, keep your voice down," whispered another. "The people who had Jesus put to death are bound to be looking for us. We've locked the doors and we want anyone passing to think this room is empty."

Silence fell. "We're all here aren't we," said John. "Well—not Judas, now he's hanged himself."

"And Thomas is still out," whispered another.

"So it's just the ten of us to sort out what we've heard. Now who wants to speak next?"

"Peace be with you," said the man in the shadows.

All heads turned to look. It was Jesus. He held his hands out toward them, and they could see the marks where nails had pierced him.

The disciples were overjoyed. Jesus told them that they were to continue the work he had begun, and suddenly it seemed as if their great adventure was alive again.

Then Jesus was gone. "But he really is alive," they said to one another. "We cannot doubt what we actually saw."

Thomas had not been with them. "I didn't see, and I don't believe you," he scoffed when he heard what they said. "I want to see the nail marks in his hands and touch the spear wound in his side. Then I'll tell you what I think."

Time passed. No one came. Thomas grew more scornful by the day. "Perhaps we were all dreaming," said John.

"Or drinking," suggested Thomas loftily. He was the last to join the group that evening and he turned to lock the door.

As he did so, a man stood in front of him. "Peace be with you," he said.

It was Jesus, his hands reaching forward to greet the disciple. "See the nail marks." He smiled. "Feel the spear wound in my side."

Thomas fell to his knees. "My Lord and my God," he said.
Jesus said to him, "Do you believe because you see me?
How happy are those who believe without seeing me!"

Jesus and Peter

"I'm going fishing!"

Peter had returned to his home in Galilee with some of the disciples, and he was going back to the job he knew from boyhood. I was no good as a follower of Jesus, he mused to himself, as he steered the boat into the lake. On the night he was arrested, I deserted him as much as the rest of us.

To deny him once might have been a slip of the tongue, twice a moment of confusion. But Peter had denied Jesus three times, with strong words to show his meaning. Peter had to face the truth—he had been scared to follow Jesus into danger.

Out on the dark, still water, Peter helped lower the net into the lake. As he sat there, waiting for the nets to fill, he watched the dark shadows shifting on the ripples.

My life is full of dark shadows, he thought. Once, I believed Jesus was leading us into a brighter, new world. Now he is . . . missing. Not dead, Peter was sure of that; but Jesus seemed to have vanished from their lives.

Peter sat and waited. The net was still empty. Blankly, he followed the instructions that the others shouted at him, but clearly they had all lost their skills as fishermen. They didn't catch a thing.

As the sun rose, they saw a figure waving to them from the shore. "Haven't you caught anything?" the man was shouting.

"Nothing," they called back.

"Throw your net out to the right side of the boat," came the shout.

They did so. "Help!" shouted the one called Thomas. "I can't hold this rope—the net's too heavy."

As five men struggled with the net full of fish, John whispered to Peter, "It's our master!"

At once Peter jumped into the shallow water and leaped toward the shore. Jesus was cooking fish over a charcoal fire. "Bring some of your catch," Jesus asked.

After they had shared a meal together, Jesus came up to Peter. "Simon, son of John, do you love me more than these others do?"

"Yes, Lord," he answered, "you know that I love you."

Jesus said to him, "Take care of my lambs."

A second time, Jesus said to him, "Simon, son of John, do you love me?"

"Yes, Lord," he answered, "you know that I love you."

Jesus said to him, "Take care of my sheep."

A third time, Jesus said, "Simon, son of John, do you love me?"
"Lord, you know everything, you know that I love you," the disciple replied sadly.
Jesus said to him, "Take care of my sheep."
Then Jesus asked him to be his loyal follower once again, whatever the cost.

Jesus Is Taken Up to Heaven

For forty days after his death, Jesus appeared to his disciples. As in the old days, he spoke to them about the kingdom of God, the kingdom that existed wherever people lived in harmony with God and with their fellow people. "You must continue to spread the message of the kingdom through all the world," he said. "But wait a while, for God will give you the Holy Spirit to help you in your mission."

As he was speaking, Jesus was taken up into heaven. A cloud wrapped itself around their beloved master, and although they watched as it swirled away, they did not see Jesus again.

"He can't just have disappeared," said one.

"It must be a trick of the light," said another.

They still had their eyes fixed on the sky when, suddenly, there were two men dressed in white standing beside them.

"Why are you standing there looking up at the sky?" they asked. "This Jesus, who was taken from you into heaven, will come back in the same way that you saw him go to heaven."

The Day of Pentecost

Ten days had passed since the disciples had seen Jesus taken into heaven. For them, it was ten more days of secrecy, of slipping through the shadows, for fear that Jesus' enemies would come and take them also.

"Now is the festival of Pentecost," they said to one another. "Jerusalem is full of pilgrims from all over the world, just as it was at Passover. Even among these crowds, we must beware!"

So they sat together in a darkened room, the doors locked.

Suddenly, they heard a noise—a noise like a rushing wind. It rattled the door and shook the flimsy roof. It dipped and paused, and then returned. . . . This time it swept through the room, bringing with it the warmth and sunshine of a summer morning.

They looked at one another in surprise, for surely the windows were shuttered tight. Then, in spite of themselves, they burst out laughing. Above their heads they could see dancing flames . . . as if the sun itself had burst into the room and announced that a party was beginning.

As they laughed, they also sang, and the songs that sprang to their lips were in strange and lovely languages that made them laugh all the more.

"The Holy Spirit has come to us, the Holy Spirit has come!" sang one. And, suddenly, everyone was on their feet, clapping and dancing.

"Let's take the party out of doors," cried Peter, and he burst out of the room and into the street.

The passersby stepped back in surprise.

"What's going on?"

"Is there a wedding?"

"Listen—those men are calling out in the language of our own province. How surprising to hear it spoken so well in Jerusalem."

A crowd soon gathered . . . intrigued and baffled.

"I think those men are drunk," growled one old man.

Then Peter jumped onto some steps and waved to the crowd for attention.

"Listen to me," he said. "It is only nine o'clock in the morning, and we're not drunk. What has happened is that God has poured the Holy Spirit on us, just as the words of the prophets promised. For we are followers of Jesus—the one who was crucified, and whom I declare has been raised from the dead. He is the Messiah, the one sent by God to save us.

"So turn away from all your wrongdoing and be baptized in the name of Jesus. You will be forgiven, and you, too, will receive the Holy Spirit. For God's promise was made to you and your children and to all those who are far away—all whom the Lord our God calls to himself."

So, in the power of God's Spirit, Peter began the work of spreading the message of Jesus . . . the message to bring people into God's kingdom of love and gentleness, and life everlasting.

Index of Bible References

Note: *The Bible references are to books of the Bible,*
followed by chapter numbers.

The Old Testament

The Making of the World 14 *Genesis 1*
The World Is Filled with Creatures 16 *Genesis 1–2*

The Story of the Garden of Eden 18 *Genesis 2*
The Tree of Knowledge 20 *Genesis 3*
Beyond the Garden 22 *Genesis 3*

The Story of the Flood 24 *Genesis 6–7*
The Flood Rises 26 *Genesis 7*
The Flood Falls 29 *Genesis 8*
The Promise of the Rainbow 30 *Genesis 8–9*

Abraham and the Covenant 32 *Genesis 12, 16–18, 21*
Abraham and Isaac 34 *Genesis 22*
Isaac and His Twin Sons 36 *Genesis 24–25, 27*
Jacob's Dream 38 *Genesis 28*
Jacob and the Trickster 40 *Genesis 29–30*
Jacob and Esau 42 *Genesis 32–33*

The Story of Joseph 44 *Genesis 35, 37*
Joseph Is Sold 46 *Genesis 37*
Joseph the Slave 48 *Genesis 37, 39–40*
Joseph and the Pharaoh 51 *Genesis 41*
Joseph Meets His Brothers 52 *Genesis 41–42*
Joseph and Benjamin 54 *Genesis 42–45*

The Great Exodus 56 *Exodus 1*
The Baby Moses 58 *Exodus 2*
Moses and His People 60 *Exodus 2*
Moses and the Burning Bush 62 *Exodus 2–4*
Moses Goes to the Pharaoh 64 *Exodus 4–7*
The Stubborn Pharaoh 66 *Exodus 7–10*
The Passover 68 *Exodus 11–13*
Crossing the Red Sea 71 *Exodus 13–14*

Wanderings in the Wilderness 72 *Numbers 13; Exodus 15–16*
The Great Commandments 74 *Exodus 19–20*
Obedience and Disobedience 76 *Exodus 21–28, 30, 32, 34–40*
The Death of Moses 78 *Numbers 27; Deuteronomy 6, 31, 32, 34*

The Story of Joshua 80   *Numbers 13; Joshua 1*
Spies 83   *Joshua 2*
Into Canaan 84   *Joshua 3–4*
The Battle of Jericho 86   *Joshua 5, 18–19, 23–24*

The Stories of the Heroes 88   *Judges 6*
Gideon and the Midianites 90   *Judges 6–8*
Samson the Strong 92   *Judges 13–16*
Samson's Final Victory 95   *Judges 16*

The Story of Ruth 96   *Ruth 1–4*

The Story of Samuel 98   *1 Samuel 1–3*

The Story of the Great Kings 100   *1 Samuel 8–10*
Saul the Warrior 102   *1 Samuel 11, 13–16*
David and Goliath 104   *1 Samuel 17*
David the Outlaw 106   *1 Samuel 16, 18–20*
David the King 108   *1 Samuel 28, 31; 2 Samuel 1–5*
David and Bathsheba 110   *2 Samuel 11–12*
Solomon the Wise 112   *2 Samuel 12; 1 Kings 2–3*
Solomon's Temple 114   *1 Kings 5–6, 8*

The Story of the Northern Kingdom 116   *1 Kings 11–12, 16–17*
Elijah and the Fire from Heaven 118   *1 Kings 18*
Ahab and the Vineyard 120   *1 Kings 21–22*
The Chariot of Fire 123   *1 Kings 19; 2 Kings 2*
The Miracles of Elisha 124   *2 Kings 2, 4–5*
Jehu's Wild Ride 126   *2 Kings 9–10; 1 Kings 19*
The Faithful Prophet 128   *Hosea 1–4*

The Story of Jonah 130   *Jonah 1, 2*
Jonah and the Castor Oil Plant 132   *Jonah 3–4*

The Story of the Southern Kingdom 134   *2 Kings 18; 2 Chronicles 32*
The Siege of Jerusalem 136   *2 Kings 18–19; 2 Chronicles 32*
The Fall of Jerusalem 138   *2 Kings 21–23, 25; Jeremiah 21, 38–39, 52*

The Story of the Jews in Exile 140   *Daniel 3*
Daniel in the Pit of Lions 142   *Daniel 6*

The Story of the Returning Exiles 144   *Nehemiah 1–4, 8–9*

The Story of Esther 146   *Esther 3–5*
Mordecai and Haman 148   *Esther 5–8*

The New Testament

The Story of the Birth of Jesus 152 *Luke 1*
Mary, Joseph, and the Dream 154 *Matthew 1*
The Stable in Bethlehem 156 *Luke 2*
The Shepherds and the Angels 158 *Luke 2*
Old Simeon 160 *Luke 2*
Jealous King Herod 162 *Matthew 2*
The Wise Men Find Jesus 164 *Matthew 2*
The Escape to Egypt 166 *Matthew 2*

The Story of the Boy Jesus 168 *Matthew 2; Luke 2*

The Story of John 170 *Luke 3; Matthew 3; Mark 1; John 1*

The Story of Jesus the Teacher 172 *Luke 4; Matthew 4; Mark 1*
Water and Wine 174 *John 2; Luke 4; Matthew 13; Mark 6*
The Two House Builders 176 *Luke 6; Matthew 4, 7*
The Prayer 178 *Matthew 6; Luke 11*
Wind and Waves 180 *Luke 8; Matthew 8*
The Beloved Daughter 182 *Luke 8; Matthew 9; Mark 5*
The Miraculous Food 184 *Luke 9; Matthew 14; Mark 6; John 6*
The Lost Sheep 186 *Luke 15*
The Parable of the Good Samaritan 188 *Luke 10*
The Prodigal Son 190 *Luke 15*
Jesus and the Children 193 *Luke 18; Matthew 19; Mark 10*

The Story of Jesus in Jerusalem 194 *Matthew 21; Mark 11; Luke 19; John 12*
Jesus and the Temple Merchants 196 *John 2; Matthew 21; Mark 11; Luke 19*
Jesus and the Great Commandment 198 *John 13; Matthew 26; Mark 14; Luke 22*
The Betrayal 201 *Luke 22; Matthew 26; Mark 14; John 13, 17–18*

The Story of the Crucifixion 202 *Luke 22–23; Matthew 27; Mark 15; John 18–19*
The Tomb 204 *Matthew 27–28; Mark 15–16; Luke 23–24; John 19–20*

The Story of the Resurrection 206 *John 20; Mark 16; Matthew 28*
Doubting Thomas 208 *John 20*
Jesus and Peter 210 *John 21*
Jesus Is Taken Up to Heaven 212 *Acts 1; Matthew 28*
The Day of Pentecost 214 *Acts 2*

Index of People from the Bible

Note: The page number indicates the start of an episode in which the reference to a particular person is found. Always look on both left and right hand pages of the episode to find the reference. You will often find the person's name, but not always. For example, if you look up references to a disciple of Jesus named Peter, you may only find "disciples."

Aaron   The older brother of Moses and a leader of the people of Israel 58, 62, 64, 66, 68, 71, 72, 74, 76, 78

Abednego   A Jew in Babylon, thrown into a fiery furnace 140

Abraham   The name God gave Abram when God chose him to be the father of a great nation and a blessing to all the world, the husband of Sarah and the father of Isaac 32, 34, 36, 38, 62, 116

Adam   The first man and the partner of Eve 18, 20, 22, 24

Ahab   A notorious king of the northern kingdom of Israel, the husband of Jezebel and the father of Joram 116, 118, 120, 126

Anna   A faithful follower of God in the time of Jesus 160

Asherah   The name of a Canaanite goddess 116

Baal   The name of a Canaanite god 88, 116, 118, 126

Barabbas   A notorious criminal in the time of Jesus 202

Bathsheba   The wife of Uriah and later of David, and the mother of David's son Solomon 110, 112

Benjamin   Jacob's youngest son, born to Jacob's wife Rachel 44, 54, 100

Boaz   The man who married Ruth and became the father of Obed and the grandfather of Jesse 96

Daniel   A Jew in Babylon, thrown into a pit of lions 142

Darius   A Persian ruler of Babylon, the victim of a plot to kill Daniel 142

David   The son of Jesse and Israel's greatest king, known for his victories and his psalms 102, 104, 106, 108, 110, 112, 128, 136, 152, 154, 156, 158

Delilah   Samson's Philistine lover, who betrayed him 92

Eli   The failing priest at the temple in the time of Hannah and Samuel 98

Elijah   A prophet of God in the time of Ahab 116, 118, 120, 123

Elimelech   The husband of Naomi 96

Elisha   A prophet of God, Elijah's successor 123, 124, 126

Elkanah   The husband of Hannah and the father of Samuel 98

Esau   The twin brother of Jacob, a hunter 36, 38, 42

Esther   A Jew in Persia who became queen and used her influence to save her people from a massacre 146, 148

Eve   The first woman and the partner of Adam 18, 20, 22, 24

Gideon   A hero who helped defeat the enemies of Israel, famous for asking God for a sign 88, 90, 92

God   Identified in the Bible as the Maker of the world 14–32; acknowledged by the people of Israel (the Jews) as their own God 32 and the Giver of their Commandments 74; the One whom Jesus called "Father" 201

Goliath   The giant champion of the Philistines whom David killed 104

Haman   A government official in Persia, in the time of Esther, who plotted to have the Jews massacred 146, 148

Hannah   The despairing wife of Elkanah who trusted God and became the mother of Samuel 98

Herod   The notorious king in Jerusalem when Jesus was born 162, 164, 166, 168

Hezekiah   A king of the southern kingdom of Judah 134, 136, 138

Hiram   The king of Tyre who sent goods and workers to Solomon for the Temple 114

Hosea   A prophet with a faithless wife, a model of love and forgiveness 128

Isaac   The son of Abraham rescued from sacrifice at the last minute and the husband of Rebecca 32, 34, 36, 38, 62

Isaiah   A prophet of God in the time of Hezekiah 136

Israel   The name God gave Jacob *see* Jacob

Jacob   The son of Isaac and Rebecca and the younger twin of Esau, a trickster who changed his ways and whom God renamed "Israel" 36, 38, 40, 42, 44, 46, 48, 52, 54, 62

Jairus   A man whose daughter Jesus brought back to life 182

Jehu   The army officer and daring charioteer who overthrew Joram and Jezebel 126, 128

Jeremiah   A prophet of God in the time of Jerusalem's fall 138

Jesse   The grandson of Boaz and Ruth, and the father of David 96, 102

Jesus   The son of Mary, hailed as God's Son, the Messiah, the Christ 152 and all following pages

Jezebel   The notorious wife of Ahab 116, 118, 120, 126

John   One of Jesus' disciples, a fisherman whom Jesus asked to take care of Mary in her old age 178, 180, 182, 184, 188, 193, 194, 198, 201, 202, 206, 212, 214

John   The cousin of Jesus and the prophet who prepared the way for Jesus' work 170

Jonah   A prophet of God, called back to his mission after being swallowed by a great fish 130, 132

Jonathan   The son of Saul, who did not succeed him as king 106, 108

Joram   The son of Ahab and Jezebel 126

Joseph of Arimathea   The man who had Jesus' body placed in a tomb 204

Joseph   Jacob's best-loved son born to his wife Rachel, the son to whom Jacob gave a fine robe as a sign of his importance in the family 44, 46, 48, 51, 52, 54, 56

Joseph   The husband of Jesus' mother, Mary 152, 154, 156, 158, 160, 164, 166, 168

Joshua   Moses' successor, who led the people of Israel to settle in the land of Canaan 80, 83, 84, 86, 88

Josiah   A faithful king of Judah and the son of Hezekiah 138

Judah   One of the sons of Jacob who helped save Joseph's life 44, 46, 52, 54

Judas Iscariot   One of Jesus' disciples who betrayed him 178, 180, 182, 184, 188, 193, 194, 198

Laban   Jacob's uncle and later his father-in-law 40

Leah   Jacob's first wife and the elder daughter of Laban 40, 42, 44

Lord   *see* God

Manoah   The father of Samson 92

Mary Magdalene   A follower of Jesus 204

Mary   The mother of Jesus, married to Joseph 152, 154, 156, 158, 160, 164, 166, 168, 170, 174, 202

Matthew   One of Jesus' disciples, a former tax collector 180, 182, 184, 188, 193, 194, 198, 201, 206, 212, 214

Meshach   A Jew in Babylon, thrown into a fiery furnace 140

Michal   The daughter of Saul and also David's first wife 106

Miriam   Moses' sister, who watched over her baby brother 58

Mordecai   The uncle of Esther 146, 148

Moses The great leader of the people of Israel and the one who brought them the laws of God 58, 60, 62, 64, 66, 68, 71, 72, 74, 76, 78, 80

Naaman A Syrian soldier miraculously healed by Elisha 124

Naboth An honest man murdered on the orders of Jezebel 120

Naomi The wife of Elimelech and the despairing mother-in-law of Ruth 96

Nathan The prophet who warned David of his wrongdoing and brought him to repentance 110

Nebuchadnezzar The ruler of Babylon who defeated Jerusalem 138, 140, 142

Nehemiah A Jew in Persia who returned home to take charge of the rebuilding of Jerusalem 144

Noah The one good man whom God chose to save his family and the animals from a great flood 24, 26, 29, 30

Obadiah A servant of Ahab, faithful to God 118

Peter One of Jesus' disciples, a fisherman, who denied he knew his master at the time of Jesus' arrest 178, 180, 182, 184, 188, 193, 194, 198, 201, 206, 210, 212, 214

Pilate The Roman governor in Jerusalem at the time of Jesus' trial 202

Potiphar The Egyptian who bought Joseph as a slave 48

Rachel Jacob's second, beloved wife and the younger daughter of Laban and the mother of Joseph and Benjamin 40, 42, 44

Rahab A prostitute who lived in Jericho and helped the Israelite spies 83, 86

Rebecca The wife of Isaac and the mother of Jacob and Esau 36, 38, 40

Reuben One of the sons of Jacob who helped save Joseph's life 44, 46, 52, 54

Ruth The faithful daughter-in-law of Naomi, who married Boaz 96

Samson A hero who helped defeat the enemies of Israel, famous for his strength 92, 95

Samuel A prophet of Israel and its kingmaker 98, 100, 102

Sarah The name God gave Sarai, the wife of Abraham and the mother of Isaac 32

Satan The name of the evil one 172

Saul The first king of Israel, a warrior who fell into despair 100, 102, 104, 106, 108

Sennacherib An emperor of Assyria in the time of Hezekiah 136

Shadrach A Jew in Babylon, thrown into a fiery furnace 140

Simeon One of the sons of Jacob, kept hostage by Joseph 44, 46, 52, 54

Simeon A faithful follower of God in the time of Jesus 160

Solomon The son of David and Bathsheba, famous for his wisdom 112, 114, 116, 134

Thomas One of Jesus' disciples, the last to believe Jesus had risen from the dead 178, 180, 182, 184, 188, 193, 194, 198, 201, 206, 208, 210, 212, 214

Uriah The husband of Bathsheba and one of David's loyal soldiers, cruelly betrayed 110

Zedekiah A king of Judah in the time of Jerusalem's fall 138